Contents

GREAT DISASTERS
REFORMS and RAMIFICATIONS

Jill McCaffrey

National Chairman
Armed Forces Emergency Services
American Red Cross

Introduction

Disasters have always been a source of fascination and awe. Tales of a great flood that nearly wipes out all life are among humanity's oldest recorded stories, dating at least from the second millennium B.C., and they appear in cultures from the Middle East to the Arctic Circle to the southernmost tip of South America and the islands of Polynesia. Typically gods are at the center of these ancient disaster tales—which is perhaps not too surprising, given the fact that the tales originated during a time when human beings were at the mercy of natural forces they did not understand.

To a great extent, we still are at the mercy of nature, as anyone who reads the newspapers or watches nightly news broadcasts can attest.

Hurricanes, earthquakes, tornados, wildfires, and floods continue to exact a heavy toll in suffering and death, despite our considerable knowledge of the workings of the physical world. If science has offered only limited protection from the consequences of natural disasters, it has in no way diminished our fascination with them. Perhaps that's because the scale and power of natural disasters force us as individuals to confront our relatively insignificant place in the physical world and remind us of the fragility and transience of our lives. Perhaps it's because we can imagine ourselves in the midst of dire circumstances and wonder how we would respond. Perhaps it's because disasters seem to bring out the best and worst instincts of humanity: altruism and selfishness, courage and cowardice, generosity and greed.

As one of the national chairmen of the American Red Cross, a humanitarian organization that provides relief for victims of disasters, I have had the privilege of seeing some of humanity's best instincts. I have witnessed communities pulling together in the face of trauma; I have seen thousands of people answer the call to help total strangers in their time of need.

Of course, helping victims after a tragedy is not the only way, or even the best way, to deal with disaster. In many cases planning and preparation can minimize damage and loss of life—or even avoid a disaster entirely. For, as history repeatedly shows, many disasters are caused not by nature but by human folly, shortsightedness, and unethical conduct. For example, when a land developer wanted to create a lake for his exclusive resort club in Pennsylvania's Allegheny Mountains in 1880, he ignored expert warnings and cut corners in reconstructing an earthen dam. On May 31, 1889, the dam gave way, unleashing 20 million tons of water on the towns below. The Johnstown Flood, the deadliest in American history, claimed more than 2,200 lives. Greed and negligence would figure prominently in the Triangle Shirtwaist Company fire in 1911. Deplorable conditions in the garment sweatshop, along with a failure to give any thought to the safety of workers, led to the tragic deaths of 146 persons. Technology outstripped wisdom only a year later, when the designers of the luxury liner *Titanic* smugly declared their state-of-the-art ship "unsinkable," seeing no need to provide lifeboat capacity for everyone onboard. On the night of April 14, 1912, more than 1,500 passengers and crew paid for this hubris with their lives after the ship collided with an iceberg and sank. But human catastrophes aren't always the unforeseen consequences of carelessness or folly. In the 1940s the leaders of Nazi Germany purposefully and systematically set out to exterminate all Jews, along with Gypsies, homosexuals, the mentally ill, and other so-called undesirables. More recently terrorists have targeted random members of society, blowing up airplanes and buildings in an effort to advance their political agendas.

The books in the GREAT DISASTERS: REFORMS AND RAMIFICATIONS series examine these and other famous disasters, natural and human made. They explain the causes of the disasters, describe in detail how events unfolded, and paint vivid portraits of the people caught up in dangerous circumstances. But these books are more than just accounts of what happened to whom and why. For they place the disasters in historical perspective, showing how people's attitudes and actions changed and detailing the steps society took in the wake of each calamity. And in the end, the most important lesson we can learn from any disaster—as well as the most fitting tribute to those who suffered and died—is how to avoid a repeat in the future.

"A Date Which Will Live in Infamy"

Diamond Head, one of the most recognizable landmarks in the United States, is a dormant volcano on the Hawaiian island of Oahu. Today the area around Honolulu is a tourist paradise, with beautiful beaches, glistening water, and luxury hotels. In 1941, however, it was the scene of a huge American military disaster.

pproximately 2,400 miles west-southwest of San Francisco, California, lies an archipelago (chain of islands) formed more than 20 million years ago by molten lava that bubbled up from the bottom of the Pacific Ocean. Over time, the barren and rocky volcanic slopes gave way to lush plant life, including an array of colorful and exotic flowers that flourished in the tropical climate of the region.

The Hawaiian archipelago stretches 1,600 miles across the Pacific Ocean, from the island of Hawaii (also known as the Big Island) to the Kure Atoll near Japan. Its geography ranges from the snowcapped mountains of the Big Island to the towering twin cascades of the Wailua Falls on Kauai. The four largest islands—Maui, Oahu, Kauai, and Hawaii—are also the most populated. The comfortable trade winds, tropical

11

temperatures, and shimmering turquoise coral-reefed waters of the islands led early explorers, such as Capt. James Cook, to wonder whether they had stumbled upon paradise itself.

These features make the Hawaiian Islands one of the world's favorite destinations, with more than six million visitors each year. On Oahu—where many of the 800,000 residents are of Japanese, Filipino, Chinese, and Hawaiian ancestry—tourists not only find the state capital of Honolulu, the stately and dormant volcano known as Diamond Head, and the beautiful white beaches of Waikiki, but they can also visit the sheltered waters of historic Pearl Harbor, still one of the largest naval bases in the world.

Ancient islanders called this harbor Puuloa, the legendary home of the shark goddess Ka'ahupahau. Puuloa's shallow waters were once home to abundant populations of fish and pearl oysters. Its existence was first discovered in the late 1700s by a British explorer named George Vancouver. In 1872 the harbor's usefulness as a natural shelter attracted the attention of the U.S. military, which considered it a strategically ideal location for a Pacific naval port. Fifteen years later, on the advice of Lt. Gen. John McAllister Schofield, the United States and the kingdom of Hawaii signed a treaty that granted the United States exclusive rights to use the harbor as a coaling and repair station for its vessels. In exchange, Hawaii was permitted to export sugar duty-free to America.

In the early 1900s the United States began purchasing more land in and around the harbor, and it constructed a dry-dock area for cleaning and repairing military vessels. Under the direction of Lt. Comdr. Chester W. Nimitz a submarine base was completed in 1922. At the new Pearl Harbor Naval Air Station, battleships were moored around the perimeter of Ford Island, which is situated in

the middle of the harbor, and a large central airfield and hangars on the southern end of the island accommodated military aircraft flying in and out of the area. By 1941, Pearl Harbor had become the headquarters for the U.S. Pacific Naval Fleet, with army, air force, and marine bases located on and around Ford Island and Oahu.

At this time the United States was not involved in military conflict, but much of Europe had been embroiled in World War II since 1939. Closer to Hawaii itself, Japan was also involved in hostilities on the Asian mainland. Since the beginning of the century, Japan had fought a series of conflicts with the Russians and Chinese. Most had centered on the northeastern region of China known as Manchuria, an area considered highly desirable by Japan because of its abundant natural resources: coal,

During peacetime, Pearl Harbor was an appealing place to be stationed. Here American sailors stroll along Fort Street in downtown Honolulu.

iron, lead, and rich, fertile soil that was highly suitable for widespread agricultural production.

In 1904 Russia and Japan, both intent on expansion, went to war over Manchuria. That February, Japan attacked the Russian naval base of Port Arthur, which it captured nearly a year later. A few months afterward, Japanese naval forces also defeated the Russians at Mukden, in Manchuria, and in the battle of Tsushima in May 1905 they destroyed Russia's Baltic Fleet. With these victories, Japan gained access to the vast natural resources of the region. Thus began Japan's campaign to rule Southeast Asia.

During the 1930s, the United States watched Japan's aggressive territorial expansion with growing concern. Its own interests in the area included Wake Island, Midway Island, and the Philippines. By moving the core of the U.S. fleet from the west coast of the mainland to Pearl Harbor at the beginning of 1940, President Franklin D. Roosevelt aimed to strengthen America's military presence in the Pacific and thereby deter further expansion by Japan. In July of that year, Congress sent an equally powerful message to Japan when it adopted the National Defense Act, which authorized the president to limit or cease the export of any materials or resources that might be essential to the national defense. America was one of Japan's largest suppliers of oil, a vital resource for both countries but particularly important to Japan.

But Japan was intent on achieving its own objectives in the Pacific regardless of America's reaction. On September 27, 1940, Japan signed what was called the Tripartite Pact with Germany and Italy, which were already allied against Great Britain in World War II. The Axis alliance, as Japan's union with Germany and Italy was called, required that the three countries aid one another with all the military and economic means at their disposal should a power not yet involved in the war attack any of them.

U.S. leaders interpreted the Axis alliance as a serious threat to their country. When the Japanese invaded southern Indochina in July 1941, the United States responded by imposing an embargo on all oil shipments to Japan. Without a continuing supply of oil, Japan's industrial and military forces would come to a standstill. Japanese military leaders viewed the embargo as the equivalent of an act of war.

As relations between the United States and Japan became more strained, all U.S. military personnel stationed at Pearl Harbor were put on alert. Regular drills kept them prepared for emergencies, but no one in the military high command believed an attack was imminent. For this reason, U.S. forces were not on the highest alert status. But Japan and the United States were moving closer to an all-out confrontation: U.S. officials did not take into account Japan's determined resolve to control Asia, nor its willingness to wage war at any cost against any country that threatened that goal.

Perhaps this view was strengthened by the ongoing negotiations between U.S. Secretary of State Cordell Hull and Japan's Ambassador Kichisaburo Nomura and Special Envoy Saburo Kurusu during the fall of 1941. While these talks were in progress, the U.S. armed forces at Pearl Harbor conducted business as usual.

On Saturday evening, December 6, the 42,000 soldiers, sailors, and other personnel stationed throughout the islands began settling in for a relaxing evening off. About one-third of them—mostly enlisted men—took advantage of the 24-hour shore leave granted by the higher-ups. In droves they converged on downtown Honolulu, some of them stopping at the local YMCA before heading to various bars, like Bill Leader's, the Two Jacks,

Adm. Husband E. Kimmel (above) and Lt. Gen. Walter C. Short (facing page) were the top U.S. naval and army commanders in Hawaii in December 1941.

and the New Emma Café. Others patronized the tattoo parlors, pinball joints, pool halls, and cheap souvenir shops lining Hotel Street. Some of the men even ventured over to the Princess Hotel to see the "Tantalizing Tootsies" variety show scheduled that night.

For those who stayed close to home in ships' quarters, the officers' club at Schofield Barracks, or the Hickam post theater, the evening was filled with music, dancing, card games, and gab. At the navy's new Bloch Recreation Center, the "Battle of Music" was held to determine the best band in the fleet. The *Pennsylvania*'s band was declared the winner, although many argued that the *Arizona*'s really was the best.

For the two men who held the highest military positions at Pearl Harbor—Adm. Husband E. Kimmel, commander in chief of the Pacific Fleet, and Lt. Gen. Walter C. Short, commander of the Hawaiian Department—the night of December 6 was uneventful. Admiral Kimmel, who had assumed command on February 1, 1941, was a no-nonsense officer who kept to himself except for an occasional golf outing or a walk with other officers. Intelligent, forthright, and hardworking, Kimmel demanded a great deal from his subordinates and even more from himself. In his efforts to prepare the ranks under his command for a possible war in the Pacific, Kimmel worked himself and his men almost to exhaustion. On this night, however, he and his wife were making a rare appearance at a small dinner party given by Adm. Herbert Fairfax Leary at the Halekulani Hotel in Waikiki. Admiral and Mrs. Kimmel left for home shortly after 9:30 P.M. and went to bed less than an hour later.

Lieutenant General Short was Kimmel's army counterpart in charge of operations at Pearl Harbor. As commander of the Hawaiian Department, Short oversaw all U.S. Army ground and air forces; his primary objectives were to protect the Pacific Fleet as it sat anchored in Pearl Harbor and to defend the Hawaiian Islands. Unlike Kimmel—a tall, imposing figure—Short was a slim man who stood only 5' 10" tall. He had spent 40 years in the U.S. Army, serving in World War I and then in several other posts before being promoted and assigned to Pearl Harbor just a few days after Kimmel assumed command there.

Lieutenant General Short spent the evening of December 6 feeling uneasy. Just before he and his intelligence officer, Lt. Col. Kendall Fielder, were about to leave their headquarters at Fort Shafter, Short received a call from his counterintelligence officer, Lt. Col. George Bicknell. Bicknell wanted to come by and show Short and Fielder the transcript of a phone call that the FBI had monitored and recorded the day before. Short was already aware of potential sabotage activities by local civilians of Japanese ancestry believed to be sympathizers of their country. He had taken precautions against such activities by ordering U.S. planes to be lined up on the airfields wingtip to wingtip, out in the open where they could be more easily guarded.

When Bicknell arrived, he told Short that the call had been placed by someone who worked at a Tokyo newspaper to a local Japanese dentist, Dr. Motokazu Mori. The Tokyo news correspondent asked Mori about the weather, searchlights, planes, the number of sailors stationed in Hawaii—and flowers. Mori replied: "Presently, the *flowers* in bloom are fewest out of the whole year. However, the hibiscus and the poinsettia are in bloom now." The message sounded oddly out of sync with the rest of the conversation, and the three men suspected it was a coded report of some kind that gave Japan information about the U.S. forces stationed in Hawaii. After mulling over the possibilities for about an hour, Short decided that whatever the message may have been, they could do nothing about it until at least the following day. At about 7:30 P.M., Short and Bicknell went with their wives to the Schofield Barracks Officers' Club for dinner.

But Short couldn't relax. After only a few hours, he drove back to Fort Shafter with his wife and the Bicknells. As the car approached its destination, Pearl Harbor came into view, its ships bathed in light as a star-filled sky blanketed the harbor. All seemed serene and peaceful. Short decided to turn in early, since he planned to join Admiral Kimmel early the next morning for a round of golf.

The festivities in and around Honolulu slowly wound down as enlisted men headed back to their quarters for the night. Through that evening, more than one marriage proposal had been made and accepted, new friendships had begun, and old friends had said good-bye. Others had made plans for picnics at the beach or shopping excursions the next day.

At 7:55 the next morning, Sunday, December 7, as the cooks at the Hickam Field mess hall prepared breakfast and men scheduled for duty prepared to take their posts, Comdr. Logan Ramsey, at the Patwing 2 Command Center on Ford Island, was startled by the screaming sound of a dive-bomber coming in low on the nearby seaplane ramp. At first Ramsey thought it was U.S. soldiers behaving recklessly while on maneuvers. But as a concussive blast hit the ramp and sent dirt and debris into the air, he realized that this was no practice drill.

On the deck of the battleship *Nevada,* Oden McMillan waited with his 23-member band to signal the playing of the colors at 8:00 A.M. As the men stood in formation, some of them noticed a group of planes converging on Ford Island. Though they saw the dirt and debris fly, they too assumed it was a drill. But just minutes later they

saw more planes, coming in low over the line of vessels on Battleship Row. The explosions grew louder and hit closer. At precisely 8:00, McMillan signaled the band to begin playing "The Star-Spangled Banner." Just then, a plane buzzed over the *Arizona* and dropped a torpedo. Before it turned away, its rear gunner sprayed the *Nevada* with strafing fire, shredding the flag as it was being raised. The gunfire missed the band members, who, incredibly, completed the national anthem before diving for cover.

At 7:55 A.M., December 7, 1941, "a date which will live in infamy," the peaceful calm of the tropical island paradise—and of the United States itself—was shattered. America was now abruptly and suddenly at war. A relentless, pounding, surprise aerial attack by the Japanese had begun. Pearl Harbor would forever be seared into the memory of American citizens.

Japanese bombers en route to Hawaii, December 7, 1941.

The Land of the Rising Sun

2

The crescent-shaped island nation of Japan—called *Nippon* by its inhabitants—is located off the east coast of Asia, nestled between the Pacific Ocean to its west and the Sea of Japan to its east. The 2,000-mile-long country is made up of four major islands (Hokkaido, Honshu, Shikoku, and Kyushu) and more than 3,500 smaller islands that complete the Japanese archipelago.

The climate and natural features of Japan differ widely from region to region, as do the local history and culture. About 70 percent of the country's land is mountainous and densely forested, and these regions are separated by numerous narrow valleys into which fast-flowing rivers and streams have carved deep gorges. Most of these rivers are not navigable; however, the surging water is well suited for conversion to hydroelectric power. Of the more than 190 volcanoes throughout the islands, 60 are classified as active; as a result, tremors and earthquakes are fairly frequent occurrences.

Hokkaido, with a population of about 5.7 million people, is the northernmost major island of Japan. Hokkaido winters are very cold, with frequent snowfall. The island's inhabitants, the Ainu, are descendants of Australoid Japanese aborigines, primarily hunters and fishermen whose distinctive features included pale skin and stockiness. The economy of the island is largely based on mining, fishing, and agriculture, and Hokkaido's farms supply much of the country with dairy products. The island is perhaps best known for its largest city, Sapporo, which hosted the 1972 Winter Olympic Games.

From Hokkaido, Honshu is easily accessible by way of the 34-mile Seikan Tunnel. Honshu is the largest of the main islands and the center of Japan's industrial and agricultural production. The nation's six major cities— Yokohama, Kyoto, Osaka, Nagano, Nagoya, and Tokyo, the country's capital as well as its economic and political heart—are all located on this long, narrow, boomerang-shaped island running northeast to southwest. More than 98 million people live in these 89,000 square miles; most of the population is concentrated along the lowland coastal plains, since much of the interior consists of rugged mountain ranges. The snowcapped peak of dormant Mount Fuji rises 12,388 feet from the central region of Honshu. The mountain is considered a sacred place by the Japanese, and its pristine beauty has been a source of inspiration to poets and artists for centuries.

Shikoku, the smallest of the four main islands, lies directly south of the westernmost region of Honshu. The island is blessed with a warm climate and is home to 4.2 million Japanese citizens. Steel and chemical manufacturers thrive along the Inland Sea coastline, and the

Kochi plains produce bountiful vegetable crops. The Seto Ohashi Bridge, completed in 1988, connects Shikoku rail and car traffic with Honshu.

More than 15 million inhabitants live on the island of Kyushu. Between 1600 and 1886, the Kyushu city of Nagasaki was the only allowable access point for foreign trade with Japan. Just off Kyushu's southern coast and stretching into the East China Sea are Amami, Okinawa, and the Osumi and Sakishima Islands. Of these, Okinawa in particular is known for its abundant fisheries and rich, fertile soil, which makes it a major producer of sugarcane, sweet potatoes, and rice.

This is modern Japan—an industrial and economic world power, far different from the Japan of the early 20th century, whose goal of conquering the Pacific ended with its surrender aboard the USS *Missouri* on September 2, 1945. Yet to understand how the events between Japan and the nations of the West escalated to a world war in the first place, it is important to learn about the long history of this ancient country.

The empire of Japan is one of the oldest continuously self-governing cultures in the world. From Paleolithic artifacts that have been found throughout the island chain—including stone tools and earthenware used for cooking and storing food—archaeologists know that people have occupied the Japanese archipelago for at least 10,000 years. From a nomadic band of hunter-gatherers, the people of this area evolved into a more-advanced civilization whose members established various communities throughout the region. Among the archaeological discoveries in this region are clay sculptures and pottery adorned with knotted cord patterns; the era is known as the Joman period, after this style of pottery.

Around 300 B.C. a new culture, called the Yayoi, began to emerge on the island now called Kyushu. By developing more-sophisticated tools such as pottery wheels, finer skills such as metalworking, and better agricultural practices, the Yayoi society flourished and soon spread to other islands in the archipelago. Initially a scattered collection of independent groups, the Yayoi eventually banded together into larger area settlements, and the foundation of their society shifted from individual family units to clans—groups of families related through blood or marriage.

One of the most important clans of this region emerged about 600 years later, in A.D. 300. The Yamato, as they were known, held power during some of the most significant cultural changes in the area's history. From A.D. 300 to 400, the Yamato population increased steadily, and they earned respect and loyalty from smaller, less powerful clans and solidified their position as the mightiest rulers in Japan. Yamato leaders believed that they were descendants of the sun goddess, Amaterasu; thus, one of the chieftains bestowed on himself the title of *tenno,* or "emperor of heaven." This proclamation gave birth to the line of Japanese imperial rulers that remains unbroken today.

The Yamato period is also notable for initiating another cultural shift—the establishment of an official religion. During the sixth century, the kingdom of Silla (what is now Korea) introduced Buddhism to the Yamato. Buddhism is based on principles known as the Four Noble Truths: that life involves suffering; that suffering is brought on by desire; that suffering ceases when desire is eliminated; and that desire is eliminated by following a prescribed path toward self-purification, which frees one from suffering and pain. This new philosophy blended well with the native Shinto religion, which taught respect and appreciation for one's ancestors, folklore, and traditions, as well as a belief in gods and the spirit world.

Over the next several centuries, the Yamato clan struggled to maintain supremacy as other clans grew stronger and fought for control. In the ninth century, when a nine-year-old prince ascended the throne, the regents assigned to govern until he reached adulthood—members of the powerful Fujiwara family—gradually seized control of Japan and undermined the imperial authority.

During the reign of the Fujiwara clan, a warrior class known as the *samurai* developed. Originally the samurai administered to outlying towns and villages and enjoyed representation in the Fujiwara court. They lived by a code known as *Bushido,* which emphasized courage and integrity above all. Samurai who did not live up to this moral code were expected to commit *hara-kiri,* a ritual suicide that was believed to restore integrity to one's name.

After defeating a rival samurai clan, Yoritomo Minamoto (seated) set himself up as shogun, or military governor of Japan, in 1185. Over the following centuries, real power in Japan rested not with the emperors but with the shoguns and their samurai. The warrior ethic that dominated this era would continue to exert a strong influence in Japan into World War II.

East meets West: Portuguese traders arrive in Japan, 1543. The contact between cultures was short-lived, however. In 1603, Japan's Tokugawa rulers virtually sealed off their country. The isolation would last nearly 250 years.

The two most powerful samurai clans, the Minamoto and the Taira, battled each other for a quarter of a century before the Minamoto finally wiped out the retreating Taira in a sea battle off the coast of Shikoku. With this victory in 1185 the clan's leader, Yoritomo Minamoto, pronounced himself *shogun,* a term that originally referred to a military ruler but that Yoritomo adopted to describe his system of military government. Given no choice, the emperor confirmed Yoritomo's title seven years later, making Shogun Yoritomo the all-powerful ruler of the Japanese empire.

During the shogunal years, from the 1100s to the 1500s, Japan underwent great internal turmoil as rival warrior clans attempted to gain power. Although the arts flourished in Japan under the Ashikaga shogunate, rebellions against the ruling clan erupted frequently, and in 1467 civil war broke out. The fighting lasted more than a decade and left the capital city of Kyoto almost completely destroyed. The war spread to surrounding provinces, where regional samurai appointed themselves *daimyo,* or provincial rulers. The daimyo became powerful politicians in their own right.

In 1543, Japan's political upheavals were interrupted by explorers from Portugal and Spain, who had begun sailing to Asia in the early 16th century and were now arriving on the smaller, more remote islands in the region. These explorers not only introduced the Japanese to advanced technology, such as guns and other weapons, but also brought a new and foreign religion that would alter the country forever—Christianity.

The Portuguese showed the daimyo how to design and use firearms effectively. In 1549 Jesuit missionary Francis Xavier established a mission on Kyushu, and by 1580 he had converted more than 150,000 Japanese to Catholicism. But the daimyo grew uncomfortable with the presence of these foreigners, and as political unrest continued, another group of warlords began consolidating power in an attempt to seize control of Japan. Under Hideyoshi Toyotomi, the clan was successful. Toyotomi immediately implemented sweeping changes: he redefined land ownership, imposed property taxes (to be paid in rice), and ordered all Christian missionaries to leave Japan.

After Toyotomi's death, another power struggle ensued, and Ieyasu Tokugawa emerged victorious in 1603. Though the royal emperor remained in Kyoto, Ieyasu moved the country's capital to Edo (present-day Tokyo) and imposed a feudal system similar to that of the Middle Ages in Europe. Under the Tokugawa regime, four classes of society—nobility, warriors, farmers, and townspeople—seldom mingled with one another, and each was kept under strict supervision by the Tokugawa court.

The Tokugawa family's peaceful reign lasted 250 years. Under Ieyasu the Japanese were encouraged to return to age-old traditions that were in place before foreigners arrived. The Tokugawa rulers were fearful of further outside intervention, believing that it not only "contaminated" their culture but also posed a threat to their regime. To stop these intrusions, the Tokugawa forbade natives to travel outside Japan and closed its borders to visitors. Foreign trade was virtually dis-

Commodore Matthew C. Perry (center) convinced Japan's Tokugawa rulers to open their country to trade with the United States only after sailing an armada of modern warships into Tokyo Bay. The lesson of this "gunboat diplomacy" wasn't lost on later Japanese leaders, who moved to close the industrial, technological, and military gap between their nation and the Western powers.

continued—Portugal was banned; the Netherlands and China were permitted access only at the tiny port of Nagasaki on Kyushu.

But though Japan returned to economic and political isolationism under the Tokugawa reign, its own culture flourished. Japanese intellectuals were permitted to own European books on science and medicine. Members of the military studied Western books on weapons and warfare strategies. The fine arts also thrived, as the government encouraged artistic expression through painting, music, literature, and horticulture.

In the 1800s, larger and more powerful nations, such as Japan's eastern neighbor Russia, and Western countries, such as Great Britain and the United States, began making overtures to reopen trade with Japan. The Tokugawa refused all diplomatic efforts—until the United States gave them little choice. In 1853, four U.S. ships under the command of Commodore Matthew C. Perry sailed to Japan. They were not well received, but Perry insisted that a letter from President Millard Fillmore be delivered to the shogun. The letter was a request to open trade between the two countries. After some posturing, frightened Japanese leaders sent dignitaries bearing gifts to meet with Perry, who announced that he would return in one year to hear the answer to President Fillmore's letter.

Perry did return in 1854, this time with many more ships and with ammunition—a show of strength meant to force the Japanese to open their ports. Finally, Japan agreed to allow American ships to dock at Nagasaki and other ports, but it would not sign a treaty agreement. Though it was willing to accept the benefits of interaction with foreign countries, Japan was determined not to allow itself to be subdued the way the East Indies and the Philippines had been. Eventually, however, a trade treaty was established, marking the beginning of Japan's exposure to the rest of the world.

The American success in Japan opened the door for several European countries to initiate trade agreements with Japan, and this development caused discontent among Japanese high officials. Though Iesada Tokugawa had signed the U.S. treaty, Emperor Mutsuhito had refused, and when Mutsuhito gained sufficient support from the samurai in 1867, he overthrew the Tokugawa regime and restored political power to the emperor and samurai leadership, ending centuries of feudalism.

Mutsuhito took the name Meiji, which means "enlightened rule." His ascendancy marked the beginning of the Japanese period known as the Meiji Restoration, a period in which the once-isolated nation of Japan would adopt the technology of Western countries and rapidly develop into an industrial and military power.

"All Eight Corners of the World Under One Roof"

3

The first challenge of the Meiji reign was to ensure that Japan's domestic advancement matched that of the West, as a guard against colonization. To that end, Emperor Meiji and his advisers had to meet three major objectives: achieving political stability, fostering continued economic growth, and expanding Japan's territories.

First, Meiji dissolved the societal classes that had been in place during the feudal period. Gone were the daimyo, and the same fate befell the samurai after they convinced their lords to relinquish their landholdings to Meiji. Though the new Meiji constitution was labeled "democratic" by its authors, in reality it gave the emperor total control over Japan's development. The emperor not only held supreme command of the military, but he also had the power to declare war, make peace, and terminate treaties.

31

He became the most important lawmaker in the new government, responsible for initiating all amendments to the constitution. Two of the most significant provisos in the constitution allowed the emperor to establish law by proclamation (rather than by political agreement) and to command the civil government and the military.

For thousands of years, Japan's government had placed great emphasis on military power, and Meiji continued in that vein. Though the restoration brought more individual freedoms, it also allowed the emperor to crack down on even the slightest sign of political dissent. Japan may have opened its doors to the rest of the world, but its primary goal was not diplomacy. It aimed to become a world power, embarking on a political course that had been described by chief councillor Hatta Masayoshi 31 years earlier:

> In establishing relations with foreign countries, the object should always be kept in view of laying the foundation for securing hegemony [dominance] over all nations. The national resources should be developed [and] military preparations vigorously carried out. When our power and national standing have come to be recognized we should take the lead . . . [and] declare our protection over harmless but powerful nations. . . . Our national prestige and position thus ensured, the nations of the world will come to look up to our Emperor as the Great Ruler of all the nations, and they will come to follow our policy and submit to our judgment.

Masayoshi's sentiment was based on a principle dating to A.D. 660. At that time, Emperor Jimmu promised his people that he would "extend the line of the Imperial descendants and foster rightmindedness." He continued, "Thereafter, the Capital may be extended so as to embrace all of the six cardinal points [of the compass] and the eight cords may be covered so as to form a roof." This metaphor came to describe the Japanese policy known as *hakko ichiu*—"all eight corners of the world under one roof"; one ruler of the world.

Japan was a quick study of Western technology, and by 1890 it had constructed shipyards and merchant ships, built more than 50 factories, laid more than 75 miles of railroad track, and established a telegraph communication system. At the time, its military accounted for approximately one-third of the country's total operating budget. The Japanese army boasted 73,000 men in active service and 201,000 on reserve. In addition, the Imperial Navy, as it was called, was also building 23 ships.

Emperor Meiji, who restored the power of the Japanese throne after the collapse of the Tokugawa shogunate in 1867, listens as a proclamation is read. Though his reign brought an end to the feudal system and established a degree of individual freedom, Meiji brooked no political dissent.

The Meiji government justified these costly expenses as a means to achieve military equality with the European countries that maintained colonies in neighboring regions. It had become necessary for Japan to acquire its own colonies, but for more pressing reasons than just to mimic the development of its Western counterparts. The modernization of Japan affected the day-to-day existence of its citizens. For example, better public health and sanitation systems helped people live healthier and longer lives, and the population was growing rapidly. Every inch of cultivable land in Japan had already been developed; by 1890 the country was producing 183 million bushels of rice and other grains, an amount that just about exhausted its natural resources. The challenge for Japan was to find a way not only to expand, but also to produce enough food to sustain itself and maintain its trade status with the West. It was also paramount, at least to Japan's military and foreign policy leaders, that the country's independence remain secure.

Clear signs that Japan was embarking on a strategy to expand its borders had emerged in the mid- to late 1870s, when it claimed ownership of the Bonin and Okinawa island chains despite strong protests from China. At the time, both Japan and China had designs on the isolated "hermit kingdom" of Korea, which shared a border with Manchuria and was separated from Japan by the sea of the same name. Each country believed that controlling Korea was essential to its own security.

Eventually the military posturing over Korea escalated from minor clashes to a major conflict: in 1894, a war erupted between Japan and China. Japan surprised the world's political powers—many of whom had credited China with military superiority—by achieving victory after victory in Korea and South Manchuria. Finally, China itself asked for a peace settlement. Under pressure from Russia, Germany, and France, Japan relinquished control of the Liaotung Peninsula in South Manchuria to China. Nevertheless, Japan's convincing victory in the Sino-Japanese War earned it new respect from other world powers.

The Sino-Japanese War did not end conflicts among Japan's Asian neighbors. To the north, another rival country, Russia, was expanding into northeast Asia and threatening Japan's own plans there. Japan also harbored some resentment over the interference of Germany, France, and Russia during its war against China: although Japan was forced to relinquish the Chinese territories it claimed in battle, the three countries ultimately divided the regions among themselves by annexing them. In this postwar exchange, Russia gained control of Port Arthur, a strategic harbor on the Liaotung Peninsula.

Japan's frustration intensified when in 1896 Russia and China signed a 15-year agreement in which Russia promised to support China against hostile actions from other countries. In exchange, China allowed Russia to build a railroad route, which was named the Chinese Eastern Railroad, through northern Manchuria, ending at the port of Vladivostok. There the line connected with the Trans-Siberian Railway, thereby giving Russia ample access to the entire region.

At first, Japanese officials attempted to curtail Russia's advancement in Manchuria and northern Asia through negotiations. Japan submitted a proposal that would give Russia free rein in Manchuria if Japan were allowed dominance in Korea, but Russia wanted to impose a neutral zone north of the Korean 39th parallel. It also wanted uncontested rights to all trade and resources in southern Manchuria. The negotiations dissolved. Japan severed diplomatic ties with Russia, and two days later, on February 8, 1904, the Imperial Japanese Navy attacked the Russian fleet at Port Arthur, disabling two battleships and five cruisers. (Japan would employ this trademark military strategy—launching a surprise attack—37 years later, against the United States.)

The Russo-Japanese War that ensued exacted a heavy toll on both sides, and no clear victor emerged after 18 months of fighting. Japanese officials asked the U.S. president, Theodore Roosevelt, to mediate a peace accord (Roosevelt would later be awarded the Nobel Peace Prize for his efforts). Officials from the warring countries met at Portsmouth, New Hampshire, in 1905, and the resulting Treaty of Portsmouth granted Japan control of the

The Russian battleship *Pallada* (left) takes a hit from a 500-pound Japanese shell during the Battle of Port Arthur, February 8, 1904. The Imperial Japanese Navy decimated the Russian fleet through a massive surprise attack—the same strategy Japan's military planners would turn to 37 years later at Pearl Harbor.

much desired Liaotung Peninsula, as well as southern Sakhalin and Korea. Russia, however, refused to consider paying Japan for the expenses it incurred in the war. The Japanese government developed a lasting resentment toward the United States when the latter supported Russia's stance on this matter.

The Russo-Japanese War had drained Japan financially, making it even more difficult for the country to maintain an equal economic footing with Western countries. Meeting the cost of importing machinery, maintaining a foreign economic advisory board, and acquiring the raw materials and natural resources necessary for a healthy economy was a constant challenge for the Meiji government. Only the outbreak of another, more devastating conflict in 1914—World War I— would change Japan's economic situation.

Japan participated in battle on the side of the Allied forces, but its role was relatively minor and confined to the Pacific. Nevertheless, World War I helped Japan gain a foothold in the foreign trade market, as the nation eagerly attempted to fill the economic void left by other countries that channeled their industrial resources into fueling the war effort. At the same time, Japan began shoring up some of its own interests by acquiring territories that had belonged to European countries. For example, in November 1914, three months after it declared war on Germany, Japan took control of the German-ruled bay city of Tsingtao in China. The acquisition went largely unnoticed by the international community.

By the end of World War I in 1918, Japan's political and economic standing had vastly improved. At the Paris Peace Conference in 1919, which formally ended the war, Japan proudly took its place with representatives of the Allied nations—Great Britain, France, Italy, and the United States. The Paris treaty established the League of Nations, an organization of 63 countries whose goal was to find peaceful means of resolving international conflicts (the League of Nations was the forerunner to the United Nations). Japan had at last achieved international recognition, which it had been seeking since it emerged from isolationism 50 years earlier.

The prosperity Japan enjoyed during World War I was brief, however. By 1927 the country was in the throes of an economic depression that was felt worldwide—and that culminated in the New York stock market crash of October 1929. As the Japanese people struggled to survive the Great Depression, a number of political factions began vying for political supremacy. Among them were the leaders of the Kwantung Army, a branch of the Japanese military stationed in Manchuria. It was widely known that Japan was eager to gain access to Manchuria's abundant natural resources and extensive farmlands.

On September 17, 1931, on the eve of what became

known as the Manchurian Incident, a bomb exploded near Mukden on the South Manchurian rail line. Claiming that the bomb was planted by the Chinese, the Kwantung Army moved into action, launching a military thrust that soon became an outright campaign to acquire the entire region of Manchuria. Rather than respond with military action of its own, China lodged a formal complaint of aggression with the League of Nations. The international committee that investigated the incident determined that China's grievances were well founded and that the bomb had been planted by the Japanese army as a means to incite conflict and seize territory. Japan's response to the findings was to withdraw from membership in the League of Nations.

But since the League of Nations took no further action against Japan's aggression, Japan simply annexed the region of Manchuria, installing as the "emperor" of the newly created state of Manchukuo a former Chinese emperor who had abdicated in 1912. In America, Secretary of State Henry Stimson announced that the United States refused to recognize the sovereignty of Manchukuo, and other countries followed suit. As a result, the Manchurian Incident and its outcome created an even more strained relationship between Japan and the United States.

Despite worldwide condemnation of Japan's actions, the annexation of Manchuria greatly improved the national economy. The iron, steel, and coal resources of the region strengthened Japan's military muscle and provided for the establishment of a large and strategically important military base not far from Russia. But periodic border clashes between Russian and Kwantung forces were common, and on July 7, 1937, when Japanese troops engaged the Chinese near the Marco Polo Bridge near Peking (now Beijing), Japan was thrust into another war

with China. The conflict lasted eight years and would eventually drain Japan's military resources and destroy its hope of expansion in Asia.

As the end of the 1930s neared, it became clear to the United States that sanctions were necessary to stem Japan's aggressive expansion in Asia. Though U.S. leaders were anxious to come to a peaceful settlement through political negotiations, they chose to allow America's commercial treaty with Japan to expire in 1940. In addition, the United States suspended shipments of vital resources to Japan, including aviation gasoline, scrap iron, and steel. Japan interpreted these actions as a threat to its national goal of achieving *hakko ichiu,* and thus it began accepting the possibility of armed conflict with the United States. Though Japanese leaders did not wish to engage in war with America, they began preparing for a battle they knew they had little chance of winning.

Members of Japan's famed Kwantung Army on a railcar in Manchuria. Japan's 1931–32 conquest of resource-rich Manchuria set the stage for its later thrusts into China, which ultimately prompted the United States to impose economic sanctions.

"I Shall Run Wild for the First Six Months"

4

Japan began making preparations for war with the United States several months before the actual attack on Pearl Harbor. Even as the newly appointed Japanese ambassador to the United States, Adm. Kichisaburo Nomura, was finalizing travel arrangements to America for a diplomatic meeting, it seemed clear to other officials in the Japanese government that war was unavoidable.

On the morning of January 7, 1941, Adm. Isoroku Yamamoto, commander in chief of Japan's Combined Fleet, sat down at his desk aboard the battleship *Nagato* in Hiroshima Bay and began composing a letter that would set his country on the path to armed conflict with one of the most powerful nations on Earth. Admiral Yamamoto was highly respected by his colleagues, who viewed him as a man of vision and conviction, not moved to act impulsively. Thoughtful and perceptive, the 5' 3" Yamamoto wore his uniform and many military decorations with the power and presence of a person much more formidable in appearance.

Born on April 4, 1884, in Nagaoka, Honshu, as Isoroku Takano, he was named ideographically after his father's age at the time of his son's birth: 56 (*I* meaning "five"; *so* meaning "ten"; and *roku* meaning "six"). In 1916 the child was adopted into the Yamamoto family— a relatively common practice in Japan when there was no male heir to continue the family name. Isoroku attended the Imperial Japanese Naval Academy and graduated in 1904. He showed great promise as an officer, and at 32 he achieved the rank of lieutenant commander.

In 1919, Lieutenant Commander Yamamoto was sent to the United States for schooling at Harvard University. While abroad, he not only learned how to speak and read English but also absorbed a great deal of Western culture. Always eager for a competitive challenge, Yamamoto developed an affinity for poker, and he welcomed any capable opponents for games of bridge and chess.

Yamamoto continued to rise in rank, and in 1921 he accompanied several Japanese advisers to the Washington Naval Conference. There, at the invitation of President Warren G. Harding, all the nations with interests in the Far East, including Japan, Great Britain, France, and Italy, met to discuss ways to reduce military buildup in the Pacific. The conference aroused some controversy in Japan; upon returning to their country, the Japanese envoys were labeled the "treaty faction."

In 1924, Yamamoto, now a captain, was appointed executive officer of the Japanese navy flight school at Kasumigaura, northeast of Tokyo. Though he himself had never been trained in aviation, he greatly improved the base's capabilities by exacting high standards of disci-

Members of the Japanese delegation to the London Naval Conference. Isoroku Yamamoto is in the center.

pline. He emphasized the importance of top physical fitness, established definitive military goals, and instituted a thorough training regimen. The result was a highly efficient team made up of both staff and students.

In 1925, Captain Yamamoto returned to the United States on a two-year tour as naval attaché in Washington, D.C. He represented Japan at the 1930 London Naval Conference, where the discussion of naval disarmament in the Pacific was renewed. The agreement that ultimately resulted did not satisfy proaggression factions within the Japanese military, however. Led by Adm. Kato Kanji and Adm. Nobumasa Suetsugu, the group known as the "fleet faction" continued to push for a stronger and more powerful presence, while Yamamoto and other members of the treaty faction continued to lobby for a peaceful resolution to conflict.

Yamamoto had long believed that the future of Japan's navy depended on its mighty aircraft carriers and their ability to facilitate air strikes during armed conflict. The fleet faction, on the other hand, believed that Japan should strive to develop the biggest and most powerful battleships in the world. Even after he was promoted to commander of the First Carrier Division, Yamamoto could not alter the direction of his country's naval construction program: the fleet faction had triumphed. By the mid-1930s, construction was under way on two new 72,000-ton battleships, the *Yamato* and the *Musashi*.

As 1936 ended, Yamamoto was appointed director of the aeronautical department of the Imperial Japanese Navy. There he was finally able to work toward establishing a more powerful naval air force, which he strongly believed was the key to military supremacy. An ardent student of military history, he was familiar with scores of offensive strategies, both historical and fictional. Among his favorite books was Hector C. Bywater's *The Great Pacific War,* which—eerily—discussed the possibility of a Japanese surprise attack on Pearl Harbor. Another favorite was Homer Lea's 1909 fictional account of a Japanese plan to conquer the United States. Titled *Valor of Ignorance,* the book was published in Japan under the name *The War Between Japan and America.* Lea's book had attracted a great deal of interest in military circles on both sides of the Pacific.

Japan seemed to be moving closer to an armed conflict with America on July 25, 1940, when the United States froze all Japanese assets in America, preventing the country from purchasing desperately needed oil and other goods that kept the military in operation. Two months later, on September 27, Japan entered into the

Tripartite Pact with Germany and Italy. Now a vice minister of the navy, Yamamoto vehemently opposed Japan's involvement with the Axis powers—especially Germany, whose chancellor, Adolf Hitler, he strongly distrusted. But Yamamoto's opinions were so poorly received in Japan that his life was threatened. For his own protection, and to silence his objections, the navy ministry sent him to sea.

As commander in chief of the Combined Fleet, Yamamoto was obligated to prepare his fleet for all possible developments, including war. Yet he continued to hope that his country and the United States could somehow avoid armed conflict. Shortly after the Tripartite Pact was established, Commander Yamamoto shared his

Unholy alliance: German and Japanese officials toast their new relationship in Tokyo, October 14, 1940. The Tripartite Pact, signed three weeks earlier, bound Nazi Germany, Fascist Italy, and Imperial Japan together in a mutual-defense agreement.

Exactly 11 months before the actual attack, Isoroku Yamamoto wrote a letter to Vice Adm. Koshiro Oikawa (above) in which he proposed destroying the American Pacific Fleet at Pearl Harbor in a lightning strike.

misgivings with Prime Minister Prince Fumimaro Konoe: "If I am told to fight regardless of the consequences," he declared, "I shall run wild for the first six months or a year, but I have utterly no confidence for the second or third year [of battle]. The Tripartite Pact has been concluded, and we cannot help it. Now that the situation has come to this pass, I hope you will endeavor to avoid a Japanese-American war."

Yamamoto's dedication to his emperor and homeland was beyond question. Like most of his fellow countrymen, he believed that his people had been divinely chosen, selected to fulfill their destiny by becoming a world power. Even as Yamamoto worried about the course his country was taking, government leaders planned to expand southward to Malaya, the Philippines, and the Dutch East Indies, areas abundantly rich in the natural resources essential to Japan's survival. Despite his loyalty, Yamamoto found himself torn between duty and reason, not only forced to confront the complex logistics of this Southern Operation, but also faced with devising the means to keep the U.S. Pacific Fleet at bay as Japan tightened its grip on the southern region.

It is sadly ironic that the man who most wanted to avoid war with the United States became in fact the architect of Japan's surprise attack on Pearl Harbor. Many of

Yamamoto's colleagues believed that the proper approach was to wait for the U.S. fleet to sail west and to confront it closer to their own waters, where their own submarines lay in wait. In this way, they believed, the imperial forces could reduce the size of the U.S. fleet and give the Japanese navy the advantage. Yamamoto, however, was not a proponent of this defensive approach to war. He believed that if Japan were to have any chance of seizing advantage over the giant of the West, then it must strike first and strike decisively, thereby catching its enemy off balance. By taking out the U.S. Pacific Fleet in one lethal, crippling blow, Yamamoto believed that Japan would quickly be free to continue its territorial expansion.

A British naval attack on the Italian fleet moored at Taranto Harbor, Italy, on November 12, 1940, convinced Yamamoto that his plan was feasible. In an attack that lasted less than an hour, the British had disabled 50 percent of Italy's battleships and gained for the Allies a naval advantage in the war that lasted for the next six months.

When did Isoroku Yamamoto first consider launching a preemptive strike against the U.S. fleet at Pearl Harbor? There is no clear answer. At least one colleague of Yamamoto's—his chief of staff, Vice Adm. Shigeru Fukudome—had heard his friend mention the bold but very dangerous plan sometime in mid-1940. One day, Fukudome later revealed, after both men observed war exercises conducted by the Japanese naval air force, Yamamoto rather casually asked him whether he thought that an aerial attack could be launched against the United States at Pearl Harbor. Fukudome replied that such a move seemed impractical, and he dismissed Yamamoto's speculation as a passing thought.

But by the fall of 1940, Yamamoto had clearly inched closer to deciding on just such a maneuver. He had good reason to feel optimistic about the prospect: the Imperial

Navy had completed its training maneuvers, which included several successful aerial attack drills launched from Japanese carriers. Yamamoto ordered Fukudome to instruct Rear Adm. Takijiro Onishi that he was to begin a study on whether a combined naval-aerial assault on the U.S. Pacific Fleet at Hawaii could be carried out. He warned Fukudome that the subject must remain in utmost secrecy.

Several months later, as Yamamoto sat at his desk on the battleship *Nagato* on that cold January morning, he no doubt took great care with the words he was committing to paper. That he chose to write his letter to navy minister Adm. Koshiro Oikawa was unusual: naval planning was the responsibility of the Operations Division of the Navy General Staff, not the top ranks of the Combined Fleet, of which Oikawa was a member. But Oikawa's role as navy minister required him to act as a liaison between the navy and the Japanese cabinet. Yamamoto also knew that the ministry was in charge of personnel assignments, and he believed that by approaching Oikawa first, he could earn command of the operation himself.

Yamamoto wrote that "the time had come for the Navy to devote itself seriously to war preparations" because he could see a conflict with the United States and Great Britain looming on the horizon. He briefly outlined his operational plan and made a pitch that he himself command the mission. "I sincerely desire to be appointed Commander in Chief of the air fleet to attack Pearl Harbor," he said, "so that I may personally command that attack force." The Imperial Navy, he continued, should "fiercely attack and destroy the U.S. main fleet on the outset of the war, so that the morale of the U.S. Navy and her people" would "sink to the extent that it could not be recovered."

Most historians concur that Yamamoto's misjudgment of the American people's response to such an attack was one of his gravest errors. As Yamamoto closed his letter with a brush-stroked signature, the gray clouds outside his cabin loomed ominously above the *Nagato,* foreshadowing the perils that lay ahead for himself, his colleagues, and his country.

A Japanese warship, seen from the deck of Admiral Yamamoto's flagship, the *Nagato*. The Pearl Harbor plan required more than 30 ships to secretly rendezvous in the remote Hitokappu Bay, then sail more than 3,000 miles south to Hawaii under total radio silence.

One by One They Slipped Away

Yamamoto's Pearl Harbor plan bore similarities to that of Adm. Heihachiro Togo, who nearly 40 years earlier had led the successful preemptive strike against the Russians at Port Arthur. One major difference between the two plans, however, was the distance the Japanese forces would have to travel in 1941—3,394 miles, more than four times farther than Togo's fleet had sailed.

The plans diverged on another main point as well: whereas the 1904 attack relied almost exclusively on torpedo boats, Yamamoto was determined to emphasize aircraft and submarine power. To launch more than 300 planes—the number he calculated Japan would need to succeed at such a hazardous attack—Yamamoto would have to rely on more aircraft carriers than had ever been used at one time in naval warfare history.

Though he played a key role in the early planning for the Pearl Harbor attack, Rear Adm. Takijiro Onishi initially opposed Yamamoto's plan, fearing that the surprise strike would so enrage Americans that the United States would pursue Japan's complete destruction.

As Admiral Oikawa was receiving Yamamoto's letter, feasibility studies of the attack plan were already under way. Yamamoto had ordered a two-pronged approach—a study of both air and sea offensives. He felt that an integrated effort by both divisions of the Combined Fleet would reduce the odds of overlooking vital details in an operation of such tremendous importance and complexity. To Yamamoto, the choice of leader for the air campaign study was obvious: Rear Adm. Takijiro Onishi, chief of staff of the Eleventh Air Fleet and the most skilled pilot in the Japanese navy. Onishi was also a trusted friend and confidant of Yamamoto's. One of the few genuinely experienced air officers in the Japanese navy, Onishi was also a strong proponent of incorporating an aircraft carrier force into naval warfare. Later, during the war against the United States, Onishi would achieve notoriety as the leader of the Japanese suicidal dive-bombers known as the *kamikaze* (a term meaning "divine wind").

Initially, however, Onishi opposed Yamamoto's proposal. He thought it extremely risky to attempt a strike of such magnitude with so many unknown variables. Ironically, of all those opposed to Yamamoto's plan, only Onishi correctly anticipated America's enraged response. Ultimately, though, he devoted the same diligence and energy to his analysis of this plan as he had to other operational directives.

Returning to his office in Kanoya, Onishi intently studied a map of Pearl Harbor. The harbor's shallow depth (about 45 feet) presented a problem: how could Japan prevent its aerial torpedoes, launched at the battleships anchored at Ford Island, from sinking into the mud before they reached their targets? Like Yamamoto,

Onishi knew that Japan's success rested with its naval air division. He summoned Comdr. Minoru Genda, a brilliant air strategist and tactician known for his steely nerve and refined fighter pilot skills.

Now in his late thirties, Genda had quickly ascended the ranks of the Japanese navy. He was a serious student of war strategies employed by Western countries such as Great Britain. As air staff officer on the aircraft carrier *Kaga,* Genda also believed that the future of naval superiority was in aircraft carrier forces, but he went a step further. He believed that the Imperial Japanese Navy should completely revamp its fleet by scrapping its battleships and concentrating instead on carriers. Many military experts thought Genda's ideas bordered on crazy, yet this concept would later prove to have been ahead of its time.

Commander Genda first met with Rear Admiral Onishi in February 1941. Onishi briefed his junior colleague on the attack plan and then handed him the letter he had received from Yamamoto. Genda absorbed its contents and met Onishi's gaze. "The plan is difficult," Genda said, "but not impossible." For the next two weeks, the commander threw himself wholeheartedly into the study. After the war, he would say of this assignment, "The attack against Pearl Harbor was the summit of my career as a Navy officer."

Genda returned to Kanoya at the end of February, carrying with him the basic draft of the planned assault on Pearl Harbor. With Onishi as his exclusive audience, Genda unveiled the nine-point strategy he had devised:

1. The attack must be carried out in complete secrecy; the enemy must be caught by complete surprise.
2. The primary objective of the attack should be to destroy the U.S. carrier fleet.
3. Another objective should be to destroy as many U.S.

Minoru Genda (above), one of Japan's best pilots and a brilliant strategist and tactician, drew the assignment of determining how to execute an air strike against the American military bases on the island of Oahu (opposite page).

planes on the ground at Oahu as possible.

4. All available aircraft carriers in the Imperial Fleet should be used in the attack operation.

5. All methods of bombing—using torpedo, dive-, and high-level bombers—should be incorporated into the attack.

6. Fighter planes should be an integral part of the attack.

7. The assault should be launched in daylight, preferably in the early morning.

8. Refueling the ships at sea would be necessary and unavoidable.

9. The plan for attack must be kept in the strictest secrecy to have a chance of success.

From the start, Yamamoto disagreed with Genda over the degree of assault. He wanted to strike a blow that was powerful enough to incapacitate the American fleet and give Japan ample time to complete its territorial operations in southern Asia. Genda, on the other hand, believed that Japan needed to launch an all-out assault that would permanently destroy the U.S. fleet and cripple its Pacific base of operation. Ultimately, Yamamoto's more conservative approach prevailed.

Yamamoto charged his senior staff officer, Capt. Kemeto Kuroshima, with coordinating specialists to address the problems of logistics, navigation, communication, and submarine deployment. By the spring of 1941, the Pearl Harbor attack plan had moved from concept to reality. On April 10, all Japanese aircraft carriers were

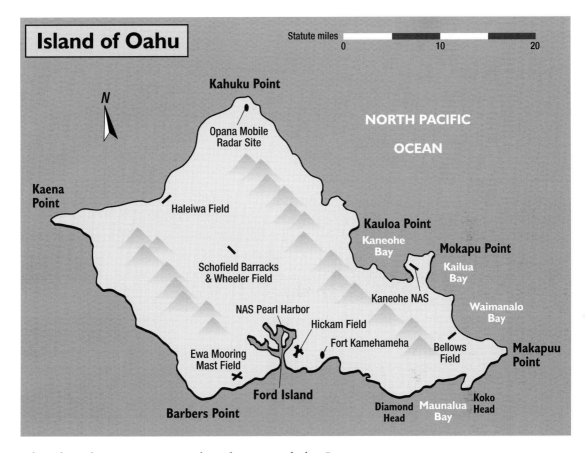

placed under one command and renamed the Japanese First Air Fleet. The First Air Fleet consisted of two divisions, each with two carriers. The First Carrier Division consisted of the *Akagi* (the fleet's flagship) and the *Kaga.* Two newer vessels, the *Soryu* and *Hiryu,* formed the Second Carrier Division. Japan's newest carriers, the *Shokaku* and *Zuikaku,* joined the fleet several months later. Combining the naval resources into a powerful task force was a significant step toward solidifying the plan against Pearl Harbor: without this step, Japan would never have been able to amass the aerial power required to carry off the strike.

Though it would have been expedient for the Navy Ministry to select a commander with a naval aviation

Because of its resemblance to Oahu and Pearl Harbor, the coastline of Kyushu along Kagoshima Bay served as an ideal training site for Japanese pilots preparing for the attack on Pearl Harbor.

background for the First Air Fleet, seniority and military protocol demanded that the appointment go to Vice Adm. Chuichi Nagumo. As a specialist in torpedo warfare, Nagumo had spent most of his distinguished career aboard Japan's mighty battleships, destroyers, and cruisers. He was regarded by his subordinates as a thoughtful, concerned officer. Even more, he recognized his limitations and was keenly aware that he lacked naval aviation experience, so he put his faith in those who did have it, relying on his chief of staff, Rear Adm. Ryunosuke Kusaka, and on Commander Genda.

By the end of April, Yamamoto was satisfied with the attack plan. He dispatched his senior staff officer, Captain Kuroshima, to the Navy General Staff Operations Section in Tokyo to present the Pearl Harbor plan and encourage its approval. But several members of the section, including head officer Capt. Sadatoshi Tomioka and one of his air experts, Comdr. Tatsukichi Miyo, expressed grave reservations. Most felt that the plan was weak and entailed too many risks. The element of surprise, which was crucial to the plan, would be extremely difficult to pull off, they protested. Problems could easily arise on the voyage toward Hawaii, during which complete radio silence was necessary, the fleet had to maintain close formation, and carriers needed to be refueled. Most important, they pointed out, Japan and the United States were currently engaged in diplomatic negotiations. If they were to attack Pearl Harbor, any hope of a peaceful settlement between the two countries would be shattered.

Kuroshima returned from Tokyo with the unfavorable news, but Yamamoto was undeterred: his plan had finally and formally been introduced to the Naval General Staff. Regardless of their own reservations about the plan, Vice Admiral Nagumo and Rear Admiral Kusaka began preparing the Japanese fleet for a possible attack. There was much to do: the carriers and multiple support vessels had to perform drills to learn how to maneuver as a cohesive unit. The air crews needed time for practice flights, and they needed to coordinate formations of aerial runs for the dive-bombers, torpedo bombers, and fighter planes. Commander Genda and his group were assigned to devise a special torpedo that would perform efficiently in the shallow waters of Pearl Harbor.

By early June, Genda had assembled flier units off the island of Kyushu, near Kagoshima Bay, to begin practicing aerial maneuvers. The bay was selected because of its similarity to the terrain of Pearl Harbor. The units conducted numerous experiments with torpedo launches, altitude changes, speed, and torpedo design. Finally, they discovered that by fitting the torpedoes with wooden fins, they could make them run more shallowly after plunging into the water.

Added to such tactical problems were vast complications over the issue of communications. Before this time, no Japanese navy fighter pilot had ever flown more than 100 miles from his airfield or carrier base. In the attack the planes would take off 250 to 300 miles away from their intended target, so radiophone communications with their carrier bases would be impossible. The only reliable method of staying in contact was Morse code—a system of audio or visual signals invented in 1867 by Samuel F. B. Morse, consisting of variously spaced dots and dashes or long and short sounds. Pilots, therefore, had to be trained in using and understanding the code.

By early August another highly trained and experienced bomber pilot, Mitsuo Fuchida, joined the group as overall commander of the First Air Fleet's air units. In July, when President Franklin D. Roosevelt froze Japanese assets in the United States and placed an embargo on oil and steel shipments to Japan, the fleet's training schedule was accelerated. Without the greatly needed resources, Japan's military would be paralyzed in less than two years. If the country was destined for war with the United States, then there was very little time left to prepare.

On September 11, 1941, Japanese top brass and staff officers converged on the Imperial Navy College in Tokyo for annual "war game" exercises. As supervisor of the combat simulation exercises of the Combined Fleet attack plan, Yamamoto divided his forces into two task forces—the Blue Forces (representing the Japanese) and the Red Forces (representing the Americans and British). The hope was that during this weeklong series of exercises, potential problems during the actual attack might be detected and forestalled.

At least one major tactical issue was resolved during that period—the actual route to Hawaii. Although

Nagumo favored a southern approach, Commander Genda, Second Carrier Division commander Tamon Yamaguchi, and Yamamoto's air officer, Akira Sasaki, all agreed that a northern passage would provide a shorter and more secure route to their destination. After two complete trial runs, two serious questions remained: was the fleet really equipped to pull off such a plan, and was it really possible to keep the operation a secret?

Many in the Japanese high command remained skeptical about Yamamoto's plan. When the war games ended, Fukudome, who was now chief of the First Bureau, reported his observations to Adm. Osami Nagano, chief of the Naval General Staff, and Rear Adm. Seiichi Ito, Fukudome's replacement as chief of staff to Yamamoto. Fukudome declared that he had not seen anything in the exercises to lessen his concern that the plan constituted "an alarming risk." Nagano agreed, saying, "In case of war I do not favor launching operations as risky as Yamamoto's proposal. I think it is best for the Navy to limit its plans and concentrate on capturing the southern regions."

On September 24, Fukudome convened a meeting to discuss the plan. Yamamoto, Nagumo, and Nagano did not attend, although many of the other officers involved in the attack preparations were present, as were members of the Naval General Staff Operations Section. Despite continued strong opposition, Genda and Kuroshima once again argued for adoption of Yamamoto's plan. Fukudome dismissed the men with assurances that a decision would soon be announced.

Aware of the widespread opposition to his plan, Yamamoto once again dispatched Captain Kuroshima to

"I do not favor launching operations as risky as Yamamoto's proposal," Adm. Osami Nagano, chief of Japan's Naval General Staff, remarked in September 1941. When Yamamoto threatened to resign, however, Nagano authorized the Pearl Harbor strike.

Tokyo to meet with the Naval General Staff in an effort to secure final approval for the Pearl Harbor attack. This time, however, he had given Kuroshima another directive. When head officer Capt. Sadatoshi Tomioka refused to give his consent, Kuroshima delivered an ultimatum. "Admiral Yamamoto insists that his plan be adopted," Kuroshima declared. "I am authorized to state that if it is not, then the Commander in Chief of the Combined Fleet can no longer be held responsible for the security of the Empire. In that case he will have no alternative but to resign, and with him his entire staff."

Realizing the gravity of the situation, Tomioka escorted Kuroshima to Vice Admiral Fukudome's office, where Kuroshima repeated Yamamoto's message. Fukudome excused himself, consulted Rear Admiral Ito, now vice chief of the Naval General Staff, and went to the office of Admiral Nagano, chief of the Naval General Staff.

Nagano listened carefully. Both men presented their arguments against the Pearl Harbor plan and informed Nagano of Yamamoto's threat to resign. Yamamoto's intelligence and natural charisma made him one of the most vital and respected men in the Japanese Navy. The commanders and squadron leaders had already spent weeks becoming familiar with the Pearl Harbor plan, and they had greatly benefited from Yamamoto's leadership. To lose him at this late stage would not only be detrimental to the morale of the fleet, but also hobble any further military operations should a conflict break out. Nagano was compelled to give his consent to the attack plan.

But even Admiral Nagano's approval was not sufficient authorization to begin putting the plan into action. The Japanese government—in particular, the cabinet—had conferred throughout that fall with the military, setting a cutoff date of October 15 for negotiations with the United States. If the two sides were unable to reach an agreement by that time, then Japan was resolved to go to war.

On Sunday, October 12, Foreign Minister Teijiro Toyoda, War Minister Hideki Tojo, Navy Minister Koshiro Oikawa, and Cabinet Planning Board president Eijiro Suzuki met with Prince Konoe, the prime minister, to discuss Japan's stance toward the United States. By the meeting's end, they had agreed on three major issues: first, that Japan would indeed continue to prepare for war while diplomatic negotiations continued; second, that Oikawa and the navy would not shoulder complete responsibility should war break out; and third, that if Prince Konoe was unwilling to lead the country into war, he should resign. Konoe and his cabinet resigned four days later.

At the prince's suggestion, Emperor Hirohito appointed General Tojo as his replacement. One of the top-ranking leaders in the military, Tojo was zealously dedicated to the emperor and the Japanese Empire. While he was war minister, he had written a new *senjinkun* (moral code of conduct for soldiers) declaring that it was a Japanese warrior's duty to die for his emperor. This was a reiteration of the banzai cry used by the samurai and shoguns during Japan's medieval period.

Unlike Konoe, Tojo was fully prepared to lead Japan into battle with the United States. The Japanese press also stressed the country's willingness to engage in war to defend its independence. On October 23, 1941, the *Japan Times and Advertiser* announced: "Japan is master of its own fate, has a free hand to proceed as it wills for the safeguarding of its own State. If it is necessary to fight America for that purpose, awful though even the thought of such a holocaust, Japan will not hesitate to defend its people and its interests. It has the power, the purpose and the plan."

Prime Minister Hideki Tojo (front row, center) with his cabinet, November 19, 1941. The appointment of General Tojo, a prominent militarist, followed the resignation of a more moderate prime minister, Prince Konoe, and virtually guaranteed war with the United States.

Though the decision had been made to continue war preparations, Nagano wanted assurances from Yamamoto that once the operation was under way, it would be cancelled and the task force called back should they be spotted en route, should they lose the element of surprise, or should the United States and Japan come to a last-minute agreement.

The Combined Fleet's task force was formidable—6 aircraft carriers with 356 planes aboard, 11 destroyers, 2 battleships, 2 heavy cruisers, 1 light cruiser, 3 submarines, and 8 support tankers. In an effort to avoid raising suspicions in the United States, Japan deployed its forces over a period of several days in mid-November 1941. One by one they slipped away, seemingly at random, apparently swallowed by the sea. Their rendezvous point, set for November 22, was Hitokappu Bay, an isolated area of Etorofu in the Kuril Islands, located northeast of Hokkaido. Three days after they arrived, Nagumo received orders from Yamamoto to launch the fleet the following morning.

Nagumo spent a restless night mulling over the departure. He still held many reservations about what this huge armada was about to do. Nevertheless, on November 26, under the pall of gray clouds and in a biting wind, the task force sailed out of Hitokappu Bay. The winter seas were rough and tossed the vessels about as thick fog impaired visibility. Refueling the ships—a treacherous exercise under the best circumstances—was even more perilous under these conditions. Several tanker crewmen were swept overboard during the process.

Most of the crew members assigned to this mission still had no idea where they were going or what they would do once they arrived. Nagumo secretly hoped that they would never have to know, but his wish was abruptly dashed when he received a prearranged message from Yamamoto on November 30. "Climb Mount Niitaka 1208, 1208," it read—meaning, proceed with the attack as planned on December 8, 1941 (December 7 Hawaii time). Thus resigned to the reality of entering battle, Nagumo— and the entire Japanese Empire—set forth on a direct collision with the United States of America, a deadly course that would have dire consequences not only for these two countries, but also for the rest of the world.

"Things Are Automatically Going to Happen"

6

Within weeks after Admiral Oikawa received Yamamoto's letter outlining a surprise attack on the U.S. Pacific Fleet at Pearl Harbor, rumors began to surface. No one is certain where the rumors originated or whether the talk was merely coincidental speculation. In either case, it was not long before the hearsay reached Joseph C. Grew, the U.S. ambassador to Japan.

Grew was not a novice; he had devoted more than 40 years to government service. Nor was he a stranger in a foreign land—his wife, Alice, who spoke fluent Japanese, was the granddaughter of Commodore Matthew C. Perry, who had forced Japan to open its doors to international trade in 1854. Having served as ambassador since 1932, Grew was well aware of the friction between Japan and the United States over Japan's invasion of

65

China and its expansion by force in Asia. Just before Christmas the previous year, Grew had written to President Franklin Roosevelt to express his concerns over the situation. "It seems to me increasingly clear that we are bound to have a showdown some day," he wrote, "and the principal question at issue is whether it is to our advantage to have that showdown sooner or have it later."

Word of a possible surprise attack on the United States came to Grew via Edward S. Crocker, first secretary of the U.S. embassy, who had learned about it from a diplomatic colleague, Ricardo Rivera-Schreiber, the Peruvian ambassador to Japan. Although both Grew and Rivera-Schreiber thought the rumor too improbable to believe, Grew's attaché convinced him to report it to the U.S. State Department. In *At Dawn We Slept,* historian Gordon Prange cites the text of the dispatch that Grew sent at 5:00 P.M. on January 27, 1941: "My Peruvian Colleague told a member of my staff that he had heard from many sources including a Japanese source that the Japanese military forces planned, in the event of trouble with the United States, to attempt a surprise mass attack on Pearl Harbor using all of their military facilities."

Since Japan had been at odds with the United States for several years, the rumors should not have come as a complete surprise. After all, Japan's list of grievances against the United States had grown each year, and the country believed that the very presence of Western powers in Asia threatened its goal of controlling all of East Asia. Japan had also taken exception to U.S. recognition of Chinese leader Chiang Kai-shek and his campaign to force the Japanese out of China; furthermore, Japan still bristled at American nonrecognition of Manchukuo (formerly Manchuria).

As a member of the Axis powers, Japan deeply resented America's offer of aid to China and Great

Britain and was angry over the embargoes imposed by the White House. Moreover, Japanese leaders viewed the U.S. immigration policy for Asians as racial and discriminatory: in 1924, Congress had passed an act that prohibited Asian emigrants from entering the country and denied citizenship to those who were already residents.

Why, in spite of the increasingly hostile relationship between Japan and the United States, did Grew's dispatch receive little attention from the State Department? Why did U.S. Army and Navy intelligence give little credence to the rumor? Perhaps it was because the notion of a Japanese attack on Pearl Harbor was nothing new. For years, writers of both fact and fiction had penned stories about such an occurrence. (Yamamoto himself had studied several of them, including Bywater's *The Great Pacific War*.) Furthermore, Grew's dispatch mentioned no time frame for an actual attack. And when Rivera-Schreiber's rumor was traced to a Japanese cook, it was all but written off. Hardly anyone in the U.S. high command believed that Japan would be foolish enough to initiate an attack on their country. Brig. Gen. Sherman Miles, assistant chief of staff for intelligence (G-2), later gave testimony explaining why the rumor was dismissed:

> In estimating the situation . . . there are two principles that should be followed: One is never to lose sight of or ignore anything that the enemy may do which is within its capabilities whether you think it is wise for him to do that or not.
>
> The second is to concede to your enemy the highest form of good sense and good judgment. . . .
>
> We did grant the Japanese the best of good sense. We did very much question whether they would attack Hawaii, because such an attack must result from two separate decisions on the part of the Japanese, one to

make war against the United States, which we thought at that time in the long run would be suicidal . . . and, two, to attack a great fortress and fleet, risking certain ships that [Japan] could not replace, and knowing that the success in that attack must rest very largely on that surprise being successful; in other words, finding that fortress and that fleet unprepared to meet the attack.

But by the time Ambassador Kichisaburo Nomura arrived in America to present his credentials to Secretary of State Cordell Hull, his mission may already have been hopeless. If U.S. officials believed that Japan would never attempt to attack the Pacific Fleet, and if Japan believed that the United States would not sit idle while it continued to absorb Asian territory, then the two countries were most certainly reaching an impasse. Nonetheless, Nomura was determined to try to forge an accord.

On April 16, Hull presented Nomura with a document known as the Four Principles, which defined the U.S. position for negotiations:

1. Respect for the territorial integrity and sovereignty of each and all nations.
2. Support of the principle of noninterference in the internal affairs of other countries.
3. Support of the principle of equality, including equality of commercial opportunity.
4. Nondisturbance of the status quo in the Pacific except as the status quo may be altered by peaceful means.

Hull assured Nomura that the United States was willing to listen to any proposal that fell within the framework of these principles. If Japan were genuinely interested in changing its expansion policy to avoid the use of force and invasion, Hull said, then it should have no objection to the requirements.

While Hull and Nomura were negotiating, two Roman Catholic clerics—Bishop James E. Walsh and Father James M. Drought—also submitted a peace proposal to the U.S. State Department in the hope that they could help find a peaceful solution to the disagreement with Japan. Hull and his staff rejected the Walsh-Drought proposal as too accommodating to Japan. Unfortunately, officials in Tokyo were unaware that Bishop Walsh and Father Drought were acting strictly in a private capacity and that their proposal was never a part of Washington's official stance toward Japan. As a result, the Japanese believed that the United States was more amenable to their position than was the case.

The diplomatic confusion may explain why Nomura did not present Hull's Four Principles to his government until the following month, and why Tokyo assumed that the principles were not crucial to an agreement with the United States. Japan did not reply to Hull's letter until May 12. In its response, Japan reiterated its position on Asian expansion, expressed its continued discomfort over U.S. aid to Great Britain and China, and reaffirmed its commitment to the Axis agreement with Germany and Italy.

Believing that they were submitting a counterproposal, Tokyo also suggested that the two countries work

Secretary of State Cordell Hull (right) with Ambassador Kichisaburo Nomura outside the State Department in Washington, D.C., November 19, 1941. Negotiations between the United States and Japan had bogged down by this time but had not officially been broken off.

together to restore peace in Europe, and asked that Chiang Kai-shek be encouraged to work out a peace agreement with Japan upon pain of losing U.S. financial aid. Neither country realized that serious misunderstandings had developed between the negotiators. As talks continued, these misunderstandings would have dire ramifications.

While diplomatic negotiations proceeded, the Japanese consulate in Honolulu was busily reporting to Tokyo on the activities of the U.S. fleet in Pearl Harbor. The previous March, Japan had sent one of its best spies, Takeo Yoshikawa, to Hawaii. Within a month of his arrival, Yoshikawa had identified a variety of spots around the main island to carry out his espionage. Aiea Heights provided a great overall view of Pearl Harbor. Yoshikawa drove to Pearl City, northwest of the naval base, where he could see the harbor from a pier and was close enough to see the airfield at Ford Island. In addition, the Japanese consulate was just seven miles from Pearl Harbor, making it easy to conduct surveillance and still remain outside restricted areas. Remarkably, information on the size, numbers, and movements of the Pacific Fleet also appeared in Honolulu newspapers. The reports regularly included the names of ships and their arrival and departure schedules.

Yoshikawa kept detailed records of the comings and goings of the ships and planes in the area, and before long he was able to identify patterns in their arrivals and departures: if the fleet departed on Tuesday, it would return the following Friday; if it departed on Friday, it would return Saturday of the next week. In either case, between departures the ships remained in the harbor for about a week. Should the fleet go out for two weeks, it usually returned on a Sunday. Yoshikawa also learned that the Pacific Fleet trained southeast of the harbor itself. And he discovered a valuable bit of information:

the Americans rarely patrolled the area north of Oahu. This knowledge was key to planning the most effective approach for a surprise attack.

Although there was concern at Pearl Harbor over potential acts of sabotage by the thousands of Japanese natives living in Hawaii, America's attention was focused primarily on the events taking place across the Atlantic. There, Germany had marched through Europe until it faced Great Britain across the English Channel, and the British alone were now engaged in battle against Hitler. As a result, the United States had adopted a "Europe First" policy and committed many of its naval vessels to escorting British supply convoys and alerting them to the presence of German ships or submarines. President Roosevelt viewed U.S. military presence in the Pacific as merely a deterrent to the Japanese advancement in Asia, not as a strike force designed to quell Japanese aggres-

Smoke rises above London after a Nazi air raid on the British capital. Throughout the first two years of World War II the United States maintained an official policy of neutrality while actually aiding Great Britain— one more source of friction between America and Japan.

sion. On orders from Washington, D.C., Adm. Husband E. Kimmel reassigned one-fourth of his Pearl Harbor fleet to the Atlantic.

Although Ambassador Nomura continued working on an agreement whose terms were acceptable to both Japan and the United States, Tokyo officials themselves seemed equally determined to continue their expansion plans. Using a complicated cipher system known as "Purple," the Foreign Office in Tokyo had been communicating top secret information to its consulates and embassies around the world. Japan was unaware that a U.S. Signal Intelligence Service officer, Lt. Col. William F. Friedman, had decrypted Purple (later renamed "Magic") in the summer of 1940. By the fall of 1941, the United States knew more about Japan's actual intentions than did Nomura.

A particularly disturbing message from military officials in Canton to Tokyo, dated July 14, clearly showed Japan's apparent duplicity. Negotiations or not, it seemed obvious that the Japanese planned to continue appropriating Asian territory. The message read, in part:

> We will endeavor to the last to occupy French Indo-China peacefully but, if resistance is offered, we will crush it by force, occupy the country and set up martial law. After the occupation of French Indo-China, next on schedule is the sending of an ultimatum to the Netherlands Indies. In the seizing of Singapore the Navy will play the principal part.... We will once and for all crush Anglo-American military power and their ability to assist in any schemes against us.

On July 23, Japan coerced the French government into allowing Japanese troops into French-occupied Indochina. The U.S. government responded quickly; the following day, Roosevelt ordered all Japanese assets in

America frozen. And though he resisted placing an embargo on high-octane gasoline and crude oil shipments to Japan, he eventually gave the order to do so on August 1, thus confirming Ambassador Nomura's fear that an economic freeze imposed by the United States would undoubtedly hasten a break in diplomatic talks.

By midfall, negotiations had unraveled. A proposed meeting between Prime Minister Konoe and President Roosevelt failed to take place. After Konoe resigned on October 16 and was replaced by Gen. Hideki Tojo, the Japanese army was in full control of the government. Roosevelt and his cabinet knew that the newly appointed Japanese administration would be even less responsive to the concerns of the United States.

What the White House did not know, however, was that Japan had escalated its espionage activities. It secured permission to sail three "passenger" vessels to Hawaii, and then used these ships to conduct more-intensive information gathering. The first ship to sail, the *Tatuta Maru,* carried agents assigned to draw up detailed maps of the military installations on Oahu. The second, the *Taiyo Maru,* sailed from Yokohama on October 22, making a trial run of the intended route for the surprise attack. Along the way, agents charted everything from the roughness of the seas to the place where they first spotted a U.S. patrol plane. Once in Honolulu, the agents continued to gather information on scheduled military exercises.

On the same day that Tokyo dispatched a peace plan, labeled Proposal A, to Ambassador Nomura, the Japanese were in the process of withdrawing all their commercial vessels from the seas of the Western Hemisphere. Nomura presented Proposal A to Cordell Hull on November 7. Though Nomura expressed a sincere desire to resume negotiations, the U.S. secretary of state saw

President Franklin Delano Roosevelt (right) with his close adviser Harry Hopkins. On the evening of December 6, Roosevelt confided to Hopkins that war with Japan was imminent.

nothing in the proposal suggesting that they should renew talks.

As the Imperial Fleet was slipping away for its rendezvous at Hitokappu Bay, Nomura and Special Envoy Saburo Kurusu presented another plan, labeled Proposal B, to Hull. In it, Japan offered to withdraw troops from southern Indochina if the United States immediately released Japanese assets and lifted the oil embargo. Before Hull had replied to the second proposal, Nomura received a message from Foreign Minister Shigenori Togo urging him to reach a quick settlement and extending the original cutoff date for negotiations from the 25th of November to the 29th. "This time we mean it," Togo warned, "the deadline absolutely cannot be changed. After that, things are automatically going to happen."

But on the 26th of November, Roosevelt discovered that Japan had sent a fleet of ships to Formosa, and he refused to allow Hull to discuss Proposal B any further. Hull then drafted a 10-point document that demanded the "immediate and unconditional withdrawal from Indochina and all China" before the United States would consider lifting any sanctions against Japan. The "Hull Note" was forwarded to Togo, who promptly rejected it. The foreign minister then informed the weary ambassador to stand by for a 14-part message to the United States.

To Washington, all indications seemed to confirm that Japan intended to go to war with the United States. The important questions now became when and where they might initiate military action. U.S. officials assumed a confrontation would take place somewhere in Southeast Asia, perhaps in the Philippines, so on November 27, Adm. Harold R. Stark sent a war warning to Kimmel, instructing him to deploy aircraft carriers to strategic locations in the Pacific. Under the command of Vice Adm. William F. Halsey, the USS *Enterprise* pulled out of Pearl Harbor on November 28 and headed for Wake Island in the Pacific Ocean. A second carrier, the *Lexington,* embarked on a similar mission to Midway Island. Despite the preparations, Admiral Kimmel did not believe that Japan would attempt an air strike. He thought that if the Pacific Fleet were at all vulnerable, it was to submarine—not aerial—attack.

Having also been advised of the grave situation, Kimmel's counterpart, General Short, grew more concerned over the internal threat to military intelligence by Hawaii's Japanese population. As a result, he put his troops on alert and ordered all army aircraft to be moved into a tight wing-to-wing alignment on the ground in the center of the bases' airfields, so that the planes could be guarded more easily.

Over the next week, Magic code decrypters began intercepting more-frequent communications out of Tokyo. A December 5 message from Foreign Minister Togo advised Nomura that the 14-part reply to America's November 26 demands would begin the following day. Because of the importance of the message, Togo instructed Nomura to forgo a typist and prepare the document himself before presenting it to Hull.

Traditional Japanese soldiers' tactics dictated that one never assassinate a sleeping enemy. Instead, one should

Japanese planes prepare to launch for the attack on Pearl Harbor.

first "kick the pillow" to wake him up, and then kill him. In that spirit, Japan was not going to attack America without warning—but the warning would be insufficient to allow the United States to make any preparations to defend itself. At 8:00 the following morning, the 14-part message began transmitting. Though U.S. operators intercepted and decrypted the message almost as it was being released, the parts were not sent in order: first came parts four and nine, followed shortly after by parts one, two, and three. After a two-hour delay, the remaining eight parts arrived.

By 9:00 P.M. the first 13 parts of the intercepted document had been delivered to President Roosevelt, who was in his study with his personal adviser and longtime friend Harry Hopkins. When he finished reading the 15-page document, Roosevelt passed it to Hopkins. The 13th part concluded, "Thus, the earnest hope of the Japanese Government to adjust Japanese-American relations and to preserve and promote the peace of the Pacific through cooperation with the American Government has finally been lost." Hopkins looked at Roosevelt, who said, "This means war."

The 14th and final part of the message was not intercepted by the U.S. Navy's Bainbridge Island Station until 2:38 A.M. on December 7—nearly six hours after the other parts had reached Roosevelt. It read: "The Japanese Government regrets to have to notify hereby the American Government that in view of the attitude of the American Government it cannot but consider that it is impossible to reach an agreement through further negotiations." A shorter message from Togo to Nomura followed, in which Nomura was instructed to deliver the entire 14-part message to Secretary of State Hull at exactly 1:00 P.M. Washington time on December 7 (8:00 A.M. in Hawaii). Nomura, who could not type, had instructed the secretary of the Japanese embassy—the only person in the building who knew how to type—to complete the document. But by the time he had finished preparing the document, the 1:00 P.M. deadline had passed.

Ambassador Nomura (left) and Special Envoy Saburo Kurusu leave the State Department after delivering a 14-part message announcing the end of U.S.-Japanese negotiations. By this time the attack on Pearl Harbor had already begun.

"Tora! Tora! Tora!"

O n the evening of December 6, 1941, while most Hawaiian residents were looking forward to a night of peaceful slumber, the Imperial Japanese Fleet task force, known as *Kido Butai,* continued to slash through the Pacific toward the Hawaiian Islands.

The fleet surged southward toward Oahu at 24 knots, while maintenance men aboard each carrier walked the flight decks, checking the placement of the aircraft lined up for morning takeoff. All the planes for the first-wave attack were already on deck, bathed in the light of a pale, full moon in an eerie quiet, as if awaiting the arrival of their pilots. The second-wave aircraft, still below deck in hangars, were nevertheless in precise order for takeoff. During the hours immediately before the attack, three major tasks consumed the air officers: they had to make sure the planes were mechanically sound and ready for flight; they needed to brief the pilots and air crews on the latest transmitted reports about the locations and activities of the target areas in Hawaii; and they had to ensure that every precaution was taken to guarantee a safe and smooth departure of all craft involved in the sortie.

Some of the Japanese pilots had difficulty sleeping that night. Most of them had spent at least part of the evening getting their affairs in order. A few pilots wrote letters to loved ones. On the carrier *Kaga,* fighter pilot Yoshio Shiga took a bath and then laid out a special set of new clothes that he would wear for the first time during the morning mission. On the carrier *Hiryu,* bomber pilot Toshio Hashimoto tossed and turned for a while, then went to the ship's doctor for sleeping pills. Aboard the *Soryu,* young Iyozo Fujita was preparing mentally for his first combat mission. He drank several bottles of beer to invite sleep, and when he woke up, he changed into clean clothes, placed a photo of his deceased parents in his pocket, and then silently waited until it was time to go topside. Aboard the *Zuikaku,* Lt. Tomatsu Ema was ready to die for his emperor and country, but he couldn't stop thinking about his wife and new daughter. Perhaps, he thought, he might be spared, so that he could return home to spend his life with his family and watch his beloved baby girl grow up.

Aboard the *Shokaku,* Comdr. Kyozo Ohashi spent the night in the operations room listening to Honolulu radio station KGMB. Surely, he thought, if the Americans had any hint that the attack was imminent, local radio stations would broadcast warnings or reports of unusual military activities. But he heard no such news—only the usual sounds of island music and occasional disc jockey talk.

Approximately 360 miles south of Oahu, the KGMB radio broadcasts were also being monitored by Lt.

Comdr. Mochitsura Hashimoto of the Japanese submarine *I-24*. As one of the 28 large cruising subs (25 had been
added to the Combined Fleet's original 3) deployed by the
Japanese in the waters off Oahu, *I-24* was assigned to
engage any U.S. warships that might escape from Pearl
Harbor once the attack was under way. As a mother sub,
I-24 also carried one of five two-man midget subs that
were to be launched shortly before the main attack. The
smaller vessels were to evade U.S. antitorpedo nets pro-
tecting the entrance to the harbor and to inflict as much
damage as possible to the U.S. fleet from beneath the
surface of the water.

The 10 crew members assigned to the five midget subs
were resigned to the fact that they would probably not
make it back to their designated rendezvous points. Still,
to some of those who drew the assignment, such as Ens.
Kazuo Sakamaki, this apparent suicide mission seemed to
be a glorious way to honor one's emperor and country.

At 3:30 A.M. on December 7, Ensign Sakamaki—
wearing a leather jacket, a *fundoshi* (a kind of Japanese
undergarment), and a white *hashamaki* (the traditional
headband of the Japanese warrior)—accompanied crew-
mate Kyoji Inagaki on a round of farewells to the crew of
the mother submarine. In darkness they climbed into
their midget sub, which was then lowered into the ocean
about 10 miles from the entrance of Pearl Harbor. A similar scene was played out aboard the other mother subs,
all of which were located in the same area.

Not 15 minutes had passed when Ens. R. C. McCloy,
on duty aboard the U.S. minesweeper *Condor,* spotted a
white ripple in the water about 100 yards to port (off the
left side of the vessel). McCloy examined the movement
through a pair of binoculars and, with the help of Quartermaster B. C. Uttrick, determined that the wave was
being created by the periscope of a submerged subma-

rine. At 3:58 A.M. the *Condor* blinked a signal light message to the patrolling destroyer *Ward,* which was cruising nearby: "Sighted submerged submarine on westerly course, speed nine knots." Sounding general quarters to wake his crew, *Ward* skipper William Outerbridge ordered a full search for the submarine. A 45-minute scan yielded nothing, so he released the off-duty crew members and ordered the men on regular watch to remain on the lookout for further sightings. With that order, the first opportunity to warn the United States of an enemy attack on Pearl Harbor was lost.

Meanwhile, Vice Admiral Nagumo's task force was nearing its destination, a point 220 miles north of Oahu. They arrived well before 6:10 A.M., when the first wave of the attack was scheduled to begin. Crew members on all six carriers had finished dressing, praying, and eating breakfast. Comdr. Mitsuo Fuchida had risen about an hour earlier and carefully dressed in a new set of red underwear. He and Lt. Comdr. Shigeharu Murata, who led the torpedo bombing unit, had purchased identical sets of clothing, believing that if either of them was wounded in battle, their blood would not show through the red underclothes and cause distress in their fellow airmen.

As they neared their rendezvous point, all carrier crew members reported topside for a final briefing. On the *Akagi,* Vice Admiral Nagumo wished the airmen well, and the men saluted him. Then Capt. Kiichi Hasegawa bellowed the order everyone had been waiting to hear: "Take off according to plan."

At 5:30, still protected by darkness, the scout planes from the cruisers *Chikuma* and *Tone* took off. Their mission was to fly over Pearl Harbor, Oahu, and Lahaina Anchorage, Maui, to verify the information the military had collected about the location and deployment of the U.S. Pacific Fleet.

At 6:10 A.M., without waiting for the final reports from the scout planes, 183 of the 185 planes took off successfully from the decks of the six carriers: 43 fighter planes, followed by 49 high-level bombers, 51 dive-bombers, and, finally, 40 torpedo bombers. At 6:20 the mammoth air armada fell into formation and headed south to converge upon Pearl Harbor.

Ironically, the first shots fired in the assault on Pearl Harbor came not from Japanese aircraft but from a U.S. Navy ship. About 10 minutes after the Japanese first wave was in formation, the American supply ship *Antares,* towing a steel barge, headed toward the harbor entrance to transfer the barge to the tugboat *Keosanqua.* As the *Antares* moved closer to the harbor, Quartermaster H. F. Gearin, aboard the *Ward,* which was still on patrol, noticed a black object in the water running parallel with *Antares.* Gearin pointed out the object to Lt. William

A Japanese dive-bomber takes off from the deck of a carrier more than 200 miles north of Oahu. The success of the Pearl Harbor attack validated the ideas of visionary officers such as Isoroku Yamamoto, who foresaw that aircraft carriers could be used to launch devastating strikes on distant targets.

Goepner. Both men quickly realized that the object was a small submarine conning tower. The sub appeared to be falling in behind the *Antares* and following it into Pearl Harbor. For the second time in less than three hours, Captain Outerbridge sounded the general quarters alarm.

The *Ward* sped up in pursuit of the midget sub until it was within target range, then Outerbridge gave the order to fire. The first shot missed, but the second shot hit the base of the conning tower, causing the sub to stagger, fall away from the *Ward,* and spin out of control. Chief torpedoman W. C. Maskzawilz released four depth charges into the water. In a flash, the midget sub was enveloped in a huge swell of water that lifted it into the air before it disappeared in a mass of seafoam.

Outerbridge radioed two reports to the Fourteenth Naval District Headquarters. The first one, at 6:51 A.M., stated that a sub spotted in defensive waters had been depth-bombed. Concerned that it was not a strong enough message, he radioed a second report two minutes later: "Attacked, fired on, depth-bombed, and sunk submarine operating in defensive sea area."

Outerbridge's message didn't reach the Fourteenth Naval District Headquarters duty officer, Comdr. Harold Kaminski, until 7:12—nearly 20 minutes after it was radioed—because it had been relayed in code and required translation. Kaminski tried to forward the information up the chain of command; it ended up with Rear Adm. Claude C. Bloch's chief of staff, Capt. John B. Earle, who promised to contact Bloch. He reached him at about 7:15. Earle and Bloch discussed the report, trying to decide whether the information was reliable or whether it was another of the intermittent false alarms to which they had responded recently. By the time the report reached Pacific Fleet commander Adm. Husband E. Kimmel, it was too late: the second wave of Japanese aircraft had lifted off at about the same time that Kaminski received the *Ward*'s report. A second opportunity to warn the United States of an impending enemy attack had slipped away.

Pvt. Joseph Lockard and Pvt. George Elliot were finishing their shifts at the Opana Mobile Radar Station, located on the north shore of Oahu, when Lockard, the more experienced of the two, spotted a huge blip on the screen—so large that the men suspected a problem with the equipment itself. But the radar was in perfect working order. Before long, Elliot plotted what appeared to be a huge group of planes located 137 miles north of the island. Lockard tried to reach several commanders to report the sighting. He finally reached Lt. Kermit A. Tyler, who was the pursuit officer on duty. Lockard described the magnitude of the blip, calling it the "biggest sighting I have ever seen," but Tyler was not alarmed. He knew that a flight of U.S. B-17s was scheduled to arrive at Hickam Field from California that morning, and he assumed that the blip signaled their arrival. Even so, Elliot and Lockard continued to track the blip on their radar screen. At 7:39, however, the planes, now only 22 miles away, slipped from the screen into a radar "dead zone."

What Elliot and Lockard saw on their radar screen was not a squadron of B-17s. It was the 183 planes in the first wave of a surprise attack. Just as the blip marking their location vanished from the radar screen, so too did the last opportunity for the Americans at Pearl Harbor to

On the morning of December 7, radar operator Joseph Lockard tracked a huge formation of planes headed south toward Oahu. Unfortunately for the Americans at Pearl Harbor, Lockard's superior officer assumed the radar contact was a scheduled flight of B-17s from California.

avert catastrophe. Adm. Isoroku Yamamoto's master plan was about to be realized.

At 7:49, Commander Fuchida radioed the first-wave pilots to begin the attack. Four minutes later, just before the first bomb was dropped, he radioed his aircraft carriers, which were awaiting word, with the phrase, *"Tora! Tora! Tora!"* The coded phrase—which means "Tiger! Tiger! Tiger!"—signified that they had achieved a surprise attack.

The assault began at 7:55, when the Japanese dive-bombers screamed over the airfields at Kaneohe, Bellows, Wheeler, Ewa, Hickam Field, and the naval air station at Ford Island. Their goal was to cripple U.S. air defenses and continue unimpeded toward the harbor.

And then the attack began on the battleships, "lined up like ducks in a shooting gallery," according to one witness. On the northeast coast of Ford Island, the first torpedoes hit the *Oklahoma,* ripping open its port side and causing irreversible damage (it would keel over and sink 20 minutes later). The *West Virginia,* just behind the *Oklahoma,* flooded with fuel oil on its port side and also sank. At the same time, dive-bombers targeting the northwest side of the island hit the *Raleigh* and the *Utah.* An instant later, bombers hit the *Arizona* and the *Vestal* on the northeast side. Vast clouds of thick, black smoke and great tongues of flame began to envelop the harbor.

At 8:05, in the most spectacular moment of the raid, another bomb exploded in the *Arizona's* forecastle and detonated her forward magazines (where ammunition was stored). The force of the concussion lifted the battleship out of the water, engulfing it in a mushroom cloud of smoke and fire that rose more than 500 feet. The blast was so powerful that it blew crewmen of the *Arizona* and the *Vestal* (moored outboard of the *Arizona*) off their ships and into the water.

More than 1,000 men caught in the midst of the *Arizona*'s explosion disappeared in a blinding flash, including Rear Adm. Isaac C. Kidd and Capt. Franklin Van Valkenburg, both of whom were standing on the ship's bridge. The *Arizona*'s band members, who had participated in the "Battle of Music" competition the previous evening, were all killed. Dazed, burned, and suffering shrapnel wounds, the few survivors aboard the *Arizona* tried to escape to the *Vestal* or jumped into the oil-coated waters of the harbor, now also in flames.

Within minutes of a general quarters alarm, on ship

Framed by smoke from raging oil fires, the USS *West Virginia*, whose gun turrets are visible in the foreground, has sunk in the shallow water. The USS *Tennessee*, hit but not destroyed, is in the background.

A crew member on one of the B-17s flying in from California snapped this photo of enemy bombers. The unarmed B-17s were easy targets for Japanese fighters, and in the confusion of the battle they also came under fire from Americans on the ground.

after ship, hundreds of sailors scrambled to battle stations and began returning fire at the enemy planes swarming overhead. Machine gunners aboard the *Nevada* took out two of Lt. Kazuyoshi Katajima's torpedo bombers, even though the battleship had been hit on the port bow and was flooding. Those who were not manning weapons attended the wounded or tried to assist their shipmates, many of whom found themselves overboard, floundering in the murky water.

The harbor was now in chaos. Bombs dropped out of the sky in all directions, torpedoes streamed through the water toward unprotected battleships, strafing fire ricocheted everywhere, and black antiaircraft bursts mixed with the smoke that shrouded the sky in an immense and eerie gray cloud. Soldiers at Hickam, Wheeler, and Ewa grabbed pistols and rifles, firing in vain at the dive-bombers and fighter planes soaring above them.

At the height of the attack, the expected B-17 squadron arrived. Unarmed in an effort to fly lighter, the bombers were defenseless against the Japanese. Once they realized what was happening, they tried to land at the various airfields on Oahu. But some were fired upon by their own comrades, who in the confusion believed that they were part of the enemy attack. Even worse, several Zeros (Japanese fighter planes) engaged the B-17 pilots in midair. One B-17 was destroyed by enemy fire after it had managed to land, and a crew member was shot and killed as he ran away from the burning plane. Other B-17s in the squadron sustained damage and casualties as well.

Once the Japanese torpedo and high-level bombers had released their bomb loads, they banked and turned south in a prearranged plan meant to fool the Americans into thinking that the attack was originating south of Oahu. After a brief lull, the Japanese launched their second-wave attack, but not before the undamaged destroyer *Monaghan* managed to get under way. *Monaghan*'s commander, William P. Buford, sighted a midget submarine in the harbor and gave the order to attack. The destroyer rammed the sub and dropped depth charges, sinking it at 8:44.

Meanwhile, at the airfields, planes lay in twisted ruins on the runways, and hangars burned out of control. At Hickam, Japanese bombs had reduced the repair hangar to rubble. A direct hit on the enlisted men's hall in the main barracks killed 35 instantly. A bomb exploded on the base guardhouse, and the freed prisoners immediately rushed to help others mount and ready guns to fire at enemy planes. A direct hit on the firehouse ruptured the water main, making it impossible to douse the hellish inferno enveloping the base. Rescuers navigated launches back and forth to Ford Island to unload the wounded, many of whom were badly burned and in shock.

A Grumman F4F Wildcat.

THE FATE OF THE F4F-3 WILDCATS

When Japan launched a surprise aerial attack on Pearl Harbor on December 7, 1941, the three U.S. aircraft carriers that had been dispatched to the Pacific were not present. The USS *Saratoga* was in dry dock at a shipyard in California, and the USS *Lexington* was steaming toward Midway Island. Only one carrier, the USS *Enterprise,* was en route to Pearl Harbor after delivering planes to Wake Island, but bad weather and refueling problems had delayed its return. As a result, the carrier was more than 100 miles away when the Japanese attacked.

When the commander of the *Enterprise,* Vice Adm. William F. Halsey, heard what had happened, he ordered scout bombers to search the Pacific for retreating Japanese. As dusk approached, the pilots saw no sign of the enemy fleet, although one of them radioed that he had been attacked by fighter planes. In response Halsey ordered six fighters, six dive-bombers, and 18 torpedo planes into the air—but in the alarm and confusion caused by the morning raid, gunners on American ships below fired on the aircraft.

The six Grumman F4F-3 Wildcat fighter planes had other problems as well. As night fell, they became separated from the bombers and were forced to find their own way back to the *Enterprise*. Led by Lt. Francis "Fritz" Hebel, the Wildcats circled the carrier but were unable to land. Halsey ordered the group to proceed to Ford Island and attempt to land there. The Wildcats approached Oahu at about 9:00 P.M., but in the darkness they had trouble identifying the island and mistakenly headed for Molokai. Lieutenant Hebel radioed the Ford Island control tower and raised Comdr. Howard L. Young, who instructed the pilot to make a standard approach to the airfield. Four of the six Wildcats fell into formation; Hebel led the way, followed by Ensigns Herbert Menges, Gayle Hermann, and David Flynn. Ens. James Daniels and Lt. Eric Allen hung back to protect their colleagues.

The pilots made normal approaches, with landing gear down and lights on, but once again they were fired upon by American sailors and soldiers, who believed they were enemy planes. For three of the pilots, the barrage of gunfire proved fatal: Menges was killed when his plane crashed into a Pearl City tavern; Hebel died when he attempted to land at nearby Wheeler Field; Lieutenant Allen, who had stayed back with Daniels, bailed out of his damaged plane before it hit the ground—but as he parachuted down, he was riddled with gunfire.

When Daniels realized what was happening, he attempted to blind the gunners with his lights by swooping down over them before pulling up and heading away. He waited until the firing died down and then radioed Commander Young again, but Young did not recognize the pilot's voice and could not confirm that the planes trying to land were actually American. Finally, through a series of questions and answers, the two men identified each other, and Daniels realized that he was talking to his daughter's godfather. Young instructed Daniels to fly in low, fast, and with lights off. It worked. Daniels was greeted on the tarmac by Ensign Hermann, who had also managed to bring in his crippled plane and land uninjured. Ensign Flynn, who had parachuted out of his plane and landed at Barbers Point, was rescued a few days later with only a broken leg.

Although the first wave of the Japanese attack caught the Americans by surprise, the second wave was greeted with a storm of antiaircraft fire.

One of the most uplifting moments came during the lull between the first and second waves of aerial attack, when the battleship *Nevada* attempted to escape the harbor. The vessel was already damaged and in jeopardy from the huge fires consuming the *Arizona* and the *Tennessee,* berthed just ahead of it. Lt. Comdr. Francis J. Thomas decided that it was vitally important to get under way rather than lose the ship. It backed out of its berth at 8:40, steered clear of the *Tennessee* and *Arizona*, and headed down the narrow channel of the harbor toward the open sea. The spectacle of a battleship cruising through the smoke and flames was awe-inspiring for hundreds of stunned and devastated sailors who saw it pass. But there was little time to cheer. Fourteen minutes later, the Japanese attack was renewed.

The second offensive consisted of 171 dive- and high-level bombers and fighter planes whose primary objective was to target the ships that had suffered the least damage in the first wave. The pilots had also been instructed to strike wherever they saw return fire. When the *Nevada* was spotted moving, Japanese dive-bombers began swarming the battleship from all directions in an attempt to sink it and block the narrow channel at the harbor's entrance. The battleship sustained heavy bomb damage and was in flames when orders from the U.S. command tower came through to run it aground.

Also hit hard during the second wave of attacks were the battleships *Pennsylvania,* which was in dry dock, and *California,* which was hit by two torpedoes and a bomb, then devastated by burning oil fires at its stern. The destroyers *Cassin, Downes, Helm,* and *Shaw,* light cruisers *Raleigh, Honolulu,* and *Helena,* the seaplane tender *Curtiss,* and the minelayer *Oglala* were also badly damaged. At 9:30, in one of the most terrible moments of the raid, Floating Drydock Two, where the USS *Shaw* and the tugboat *Sotoyomo* were docked, took five bombs and erupted in a ball of flame. The raging fires ignited the *Shaw*'s forward magazines, and the ship exploded like a fireworks factory in a blast so powerful that it severed the bow of the ship.

Shortly after that, the last of the Japanese planes flew off. The relentless bombing raid was finally over, leaving Pearl Harbor and the U.S. Pacific Fleet an indescribable mass of devastation. Of the eight battleships in port that morning, five were either sunk or severely damaged. Oahu air bases also sustained heavy losses, including 87 navy aircraft and 63 Hawaiian Air Force craft. And the number of casualties was staggering: as many as 2,403 dead—almost half of them on the *Arizona*—and 1,178 wounded. Some damaged ships had capsized, trapping

Sailors and marines on shore watch helplessly as their comrades scramble to abandon the *California,* which has been hit by two torpedoes and a bomb and is burning at the stern.

crew members alive in watertight tombs.

Japanese casualties were much lighter: about 129 dead, including 55 airmen and 9 of the 10 crewmen aboard the midget submarines. The only midget sub survivor was Ens. Kazuo Sakamaki, who abandoned his damaged vessel and washed ashore near Bellows Field. Sakamaki became the first Japanese prisoner of war. Of the more than 350 Japanese planes that took part in the attack on Pearl Harbor, only 29 were lost. Half of the Japanese fatalities resulted from the sinking of submarine *I-70.* By 1:30 P.M., the Imperial Japanese Fleet task force was already sailing north away from Hawaii.

Early in the attack Admiral Kimmel had watched in horror from Commander in Chief, Pacific (CINCPAC) Headquarters on the submarine base as his fleet was decimated by the enemy raid. Seeing the majestic battle-ships blown apart was difficult enough, but what grieved Kimmel most was the chilling fact that the men for whom he was responsible were suffering and dying. To Kimmel, these men were not nameless uniforms; he knew thousands of them by sight, hundreds by name, and many personally.

As Kimmel watched, a spent .50 caliber machine-gun bullet crashed through the window where he stood. Though it struck him on the chest, it caused no harm; instead, it simply dropped to the floor, leaving little more than a black splotch on his otherwise spotless white uniform. Kimmel sighed as he picked up the bullet. "It would have been merciful had it killed me," he said.

Remember
Pearl Harbor

At Pearl Harbor, America discovered the high cost of being caught unprepared.

In the first few hours after the Japanese planes vanished from sight, both the military personnel and the civilian population on Oahu wrestled with a flood of emotions—fear, grief, disbelief, anguish. Though the Japanese had focused their attack on the U.S. air and naval forces, the city of Honolulu also suffered property damage and human casualties. Defective American antiaircraft shells rained down on city streets, demolishing buildings and igniting fires.

In the tumult that followed the surprise attack, frightening rumors spread quickly among soldiers, sailors, and civilians: that the Japanese were about to execute yet another strike; that Oahu had been invaded; that enemy paratroopers were landing in Waikiki; that enemy troops were in the process of occupying the island; that the island's drinking water had been poisoned. Others even claimed that San Francisco, California, was under attack or that Japanese laborers had cut arrows in the sugarcane fields that pointed to the harbor and directed enemy aircraft to their targets.

As the day wore on, the tales became even wilder. In the aftermath of the morning attack, anything seemed possible. Some who were still bewildered by what had happened wondered whether the attack had been no more than a series of military maneuvers and practice drills gone terribly awry. Webley Edwards, a disc jockey for Honolulu radio station KGMB, busily fielded calls from doubtful listeners. Finally, exasperated by the calls, Edwards announced over and over on the air that the attack was "the real McCoy." Many of those who listened to the radio that day to find out exactly what had happened still remember Edwards's unforgettable words.

In the wake of the raid, Pearl Harbor was immersed in a frenzy of activity. The death and devastation was overwhelming. Battleships, destroyers, and cruisers listed or were overturned in the muddy harbor water. Personnel who had not been injured scrambled about, putting out fires on ships and at the airfields, where aircraft had been lined up wing to wing for security reasons. A seemingly endless stream of rescue boats pulled up to Ford Island's seaplane ramp to drop off hundreds of wounded crewmen. Some of them were barely alive; the only thing left to do for these men was to administer injections of morphine to ease their pain. The more fortunate ones, though they arrived burned and maimed from the onslaught, would survive their injuries.

Service and support personnel who had not been present during the attack began flooding into the base, reporting to their assigned posts or assisting medical personnel as they converted undamaged barracks into temporary infirmaries. Along Battleship Row, rescue efforts were under way to free dozens of trapped crewmen on the overturned USS *Oklahoma, West Virginia, California,* and other ships. Rescue crews grabbed hammers and wrenches and banged on the ships' hulls, hoping for a tapping reply that signaled someone was still alive. When they heard a reply, they repeated the banging, following the tapping until they reached the trapped men. The first two men, pulled out of the *Oklahoma,* didn't make it: they were accidentally asphyxiated when the acetylene torch used to cut through the metal consumed all their oxygen.

Working well into the evening, officers and enlisted men attempted to douse the fires that still raged aboard the crippled battleships. Most of their work was futile, however: the *Arizona* burned for two days after the attack. The crewmen on the *West Virginia,* though they fought the fires valiantly until about 5:00 that evening, finally gave up and abandoned the ship. But the fire continued to burn out of control, and three men remained trapped below in the pump room. The sailors held on for 16 days, hoping to see the faces of rescuers. They never did.

Despite such tragedies, countless stories of heroism emerged from the devastation wrought by the attack. One crew, after working for almost 36 hours, wrenched free 32 survivors from the *Oklahoma*'s hull. Aboard the hospital ship *Solace,* crew members remained to help about three dozen men from the *West Virginia* who were forced overboard by an explosion, despite the impending danger of more explosions. S1c. James V. Saccavino was forced to dive overboard to douse his burning clothes after he maneuvered his launch directly into the flaming, oil-covered water to rescue men trapped by the inferno.

A large complement of civilian workers who lived and worked at the naval installation joined the military personnel to rescue the wounded, fight fires, and even refit and arm ships with antiaircraft weapons in the event

America's armed forces found heroes amid the Pearl Harbor disaster. This page: Pilots Kenneth Taylor and George Welch, who took off from Haleiwa Field and managed to shoot down seven Japanese planes. Opposite page: Mess attendant Doris Miller, here being awarded the Navy Cross, manned an antiaircraft gun on the *West Virginia* at the height of the attack.

another attack came. Pipe fitter Bernard Linberg dove into the harbor waters to save a sailor who appeared to be drowning. Workers from Shop 70 constructed additional stretchers for the many wounded arriving at Ford Island. And in Shop 51, civilian Elmer Perry set up a makeshift emergency first aid center.

Though the Japanese pilots owned the airspace over Pearl Harbor during the first wave of the surprise attack, several American pilots had managed to get airborne. Two pilots, Lieutenants Kenneth Taylor and George Welch, were stationed at the small Haleiwa airfield on the west side of Oahu. They had gone to Pearl Harbor for the weekly Saturday evening dance and then found their way to an all-night poker game. They were still there when the attack began. Welch called ahead to Haleiwa and ordered the crew to have their planes ready for

takeoff. He and Taylor raced to Taylor's car and sped away, harassed by the strafing fire of a Japanese Zero.

The two pilots were in the air just as the first wave was ending. They flew up behind 12 Japanese planes retreating after their attack on Ewa Field and shot down two of them before heading back to Wheeler to refuel and rearm. Welch and Taylor took to the skies again, joined by other American pilots, at about 9:00 A.M. Even after Taylor was wounded in the left arm and leg, he continued fighting the Japanese, until both men ran out of ammunition once more and returned to Wheeler. The two lieutenants were credited with downing seven Japanese planes. For his efforts, Lieutenant Taylor was awarded the Purple Heart, and four other army fighter pilots received decorations for valor, including the distinguished Silver Star.

In all, the men who entered combat against the Japanese that day earned 16 Medals of Honor (a highly prestigious decoration awarded in the name of the U.S. Congress). Eleven of them were awarded posthumously. Among the recipients were three officers from the *Arizona*: Rear Adm. Isaac C. Kidd and Capt. Franklin Van Valkenburg, who were killed when the ship's forward magazines exploded, and Lt. Comdr. Samuel Glenn Fuqua, who led the fire fighting on deck and supervised the removal of the wounded. Fuqua was also the officer who gave the order to abandon ship when the sinking vessel appeared unsalvageable.

Doris Miller, a mess attendant, was the first black man to be awarded the Navy Cross for his acts of heroism in battle. As the *West Virginia* came under attack, Miller went above deck to help his shipmates and skipper, Capt. Mervyn Bennion, who had been mortally wounded. After Bennion died, Miller—with no training—manned a machine gun on the conning tower and began firing at the Japanese planes swarming the ship.

At sunset on December 7, 1941, bugles sounded evening colors in a routine ceremony that continued despite the horrific events of that morning. On Oahu, military personnel found comfort in hearing the colors: America had survived a horrible attack and remained a free nation. But whether that would continue to be the case weighed heavily on the minds of hundreds of soldiers, sailors, marines, and civilians that night as they sat in the darkness and quiet of an island that had been ordered to maintain blackout conditions.

Earlier in the day, at the insistence of General Short and backed by President Roosevelt himself, Hawaiian territorial governor Joseph Poindexter had placed Hawaii under martial law. This declaration shifted power from Hawaiian civilian authority to a military governor and

President Roosevelt addresses Congress and asks for a declaration of war on Japan, December 8, 1941.

allowed Short to impose restrictions and bans as he felt necessary, including strict mandatory curfews and black-outs, press censorship, prohibition of liquor sales, and the suspension of civilian courts. Until martial law was lifted, criminal offenses ranging from murder to curfew violations would be prosecuted by army officers in military provost courts. Hawaii would remain under martial law until October 1944.

More-serious ramifications of the attack came the following day. On December 8, at approximately 12:20 P.M. Washington time, President Roosevelt, assisted by his son Jimmy, entered the packed chamber of the House of Representatives to deliver a war message to the highest-ranking government and military officials:

Yesterday, December 7, 1941—a date which will live in infamy—the United States of America was suddenly and deliberately attacked by naval and air forces of the Empire of Japan. The United States was at peace with the Nation and, at the solicitation of Japan, was still in conversation with its Government and its Emperor looking toward the maintenance of peace in the Pacific. . . .

Always will we remember the character of the onslaught against us. No matter how long it may take us to overcome this premeditated invasion, the American people in their righteous might will win through absolute victory. . . .

I ask that Congress declare that since the unprovoked and dastardly attack by Japan on Sunday, December seventh, a state of war has existed between the United States and the Japanese Empire.

Roosevelt's speech lasted only six minutes. In less than one hour, Congress voted to declare war against Japan. America's isolationism had ended.

Now that the country was officially at war, rebuilding the U.S. Pacific Fleet became even more important. In the days following the attack on Pearl Harbor, the public openly questioned how the United States could have been caught so tragically off guard.

After assessing the damage at Oahu, however, U.S. officials realized that the Japanese attack could have done far more harm. None of the aircraft carriers had been in port, and therefore they were spared entirely. The shore repair facilities and the tank farms, which held thousands of gallons of oil imported from the mainland, had been completely overlooked in the raid. And since the channel remained unblocked, Pearl Harbor could continue as a naval base. The shallow waters of the harbor, which had

caused such concern among the Japanese bombing crews, also allowed Americans to refloat and repair many of the damaged ships; had they been sunk in the open sea, they would have been lost forever.

Salvage and repair operations were under way almost immediately and were swiftly completed. The USS *Pennsylvania, Maryland,* and *Tennessee* were available for action just two weeks after the attack. The USS *Nevada* was returned to active service before the end of 1942, and the *California* by the spring of 1943. Incredibly, only two battleships, the *Arizona* and the *Oklahoma,* were completely lost. The army's cleanup and repair projects were much less arduous than those of the navy. Many of the planes destroyed during the raid were old or obsolete, limiting the salvage operations. The airfields were repaired and resurfaced, and hangars and barracks were reconstructed with little difficulty.

The opening of congressional hearings on Pearl Harbor. In all, five official investigations probed the causes of the disaster.

THE USS *ARIZONA* MEMORIAL

Years after [the ship] sank to the harbor bottom, the Arizona's *fuel bunkers are still leaking. When the droplets hit the air a few feet above us, they lose form, becoming part of the slick that bobs on the waves under the gaze of the onlookers standing in the memorial. . . . There is a sense that the* Arizona, *which is easy to [imagine as human] anyway, is still bleeding slightly from one of its wounds.*

—Daniel J. Lenihan of the National Park Service
after diving in the ruins of the *Arizona*, 1983

The moment of death for the mighty battleship *Arizona* came at 8:10 A.M. on December 7, 1941, when a 1,760-pound bomb pierced the ship's forward deck, igniting more than one million pounds of ammunition. The resulting explosion ripped open the ship as though it were a tin can. Flames engulfed it as it sank, taking with it 1,177 of 1,553 crew members.

The *Arizona* burned for two days. In the immediate aftermath of the attack, the U.S. Navy tried to assess the damage to the base and repair as many of its battleships as possible. It was clear to those surveying the destruction, however, that the *Arizona*, which had sunk to the bottom of the 40-foot harbor, would never sail again. The navy salvaged the vessel's masts and superstructure for scrap and moved the two rear turrets to battery sites onshore. At first the navy wanted to raise the ship to remove the remains of the dead, but medical examiners advised against it, explaining that most of the men who had been caught in the blast had been either cremated or burned beyond recognition. And so, following a long-standing naval tradition of burying at sea those who died there, the remains were left undisturbed.

As early as 1943, a civilian worker at Pearl Harbor proposed that a memorial be built to honor the men who died in the attack. The idea sparked the interest of Hawaii veterans and other patriotic groups, who began organizing fund-raisers to pay for the cost of erecting such a structure. In 1950 Adm. Arthur Radford, commander in chief of the Pacific Fleet, had a flag raised over the sunken ship's severed main mast. Eight years later, President Dwight D. Eisenhower authorized the creation of a national memorial on the site. With federal funds and donations from private citizens, the USS *Arizona* Memorial was completed in 1961 and dedicated on Memorial Day 1962.

Today the memorial is maintained by the National Park Service. The 184-foot curved structure straddles the ship transversely above the waterline without touching any part of the original vessel. It was envisioned by

The USS Arizona *Memorial in Pearl Harbor. The outline of the sunken ship, on which 1,177 American seamen perished, is visible beneath the surface of the water.*

architect Alfred Preis to symbolize triumph rising from initial defeat. "The overall effect is one of serenity," Preis explained. "Overtones of sadness have been omitted to permit the individual to contemplate his own personal responses." Twenty-one large openings in the sides and roof of the building represent the traditional 21-gun salute to deceased members of the military.

Each year, thousands of tourists visit the USS *Arizona* Memorial, where a visitors' center displays photographs and artifacts of the battleship, and a ferry takes guests across the water to the memorial building. Perhaps the most vivid reminder of the *Arizona*'s place in history is in the shrine room of the memorial. There, carved on a marble wall, are the names and ranks of the 1,177 crewmen who went down with their ship. The list stands as a lasting testament to the tragic consequences of war.

On December 17, 1941, Adm. Husband E. Kimmel and Lt. Gen. Walter C. Short were relieved of their commands, for failure to "be on alert," by Secretary of the Navy Frank Knox and Secretary of War Henry Stimson, respectively. Kimmel's permanent replacement was Adm. Chester W. Nimitz; Short was replaced as commander of the Hawaiian Department by Lt. Gen. Delos C. Emmons. In all, five military investigations were conducted to determine how the Japanese could so successfully take the American fleet unaware. President Roosevelt himself appointed the first investigating committee, named the Roberts Commission after its chairman, Supreme Court justice Owen Roberts. The commission conducted its investigation in Hawaii and Washington during December 1941 and January 1942.

In its final report, the Roberts Commission concluded that a series of "errors in judgment" and "dereliction of duty" on the part of Kimmel and Short allowed the Japanese to successfully launch a surprise attack on Pearl Harbor. Omitted from the report was any mention of the top secret Magic decryption program or the information that code breakers obtained when they intercepted messages between Tokyo and the Japanese consul in Honolulu. Though the report also placed blame on unnamed Washington officials for many of the "causes contributory to the success of the Japanese," both Kimmel and Short were ultimately taken to task for the attack.

Although neither man was formally charged, their reputations were permanently damaged by the report. Short "retired" on February 28, 1942, and joined the Ford Motor Company in Dallas, Texas, whose factory had been converted to manufacture war materials. He died in 1949. Kimmel left the military on March 1, 1942, and later joined the shipbuilding firm of Frederick R. Harris as a consultant. He continued campaigning to exonerate himself until his death in 1968.

In May 1999, the U.S. Senate passed a resolution requesting that President Bill Clinton excuse Admiral Kimmel and Major General Short of blame for the attack on Pearl Harbor. The Senate also requested that the two men be posthumously promoted, in part because crucial information (such as that received in the decoded diplomatic messages) may have been withheld from them by the U.S. government. Although several retired senior naval officers agreed with the Senate's resolution, many others believed that Kimmel and Short were justifiably punished.

In the aftermath of the surprise attack, Americans struggled to contain their fury over the treachery of the Japanese. An ugly form of racism emerged. On February 19, 1942, in one of the most controversial ramifications of the Pearl Harbor attack, President Roosevelt declared in Executive Order 9066 that "by virtue of their racial similarity to the enemy," all Japanese men, women, and children living in America were to be evacuated from their homes and interned. Japanese-Americans were suddenly considered a "national security risk." Forced to abandon their homes, property, and businesses, more than 110,000 Japanese (70,000 of whom were citizens of the United States) were relocated to 10 camps scattered throughout desert areas in Utah, Arizona, Colorado, Wyoming, Idaho, Arkansas, and California. The camps remained in force until 1945.

A Japanese-American mother and children, tagged for identification, wait to be shipped to an internment camp, March 1942. Although there were no recorded incidents of espionage or sabotage by Japanese-Americans during World War II, officials justified the internment program in the name of national security.

The body of a sailor, one of America's first casualties of World War II, washes ashore on an Oahu beach. The terrible conflict that began at Pearl Harbor would consume millions of other American and Japanese lives before the fighting finally ended nearly four years later.

Among those who were interned in these camps were Senator Daniel Inouye of Hawaii, actor George Takei (who played Sulu on the original *Star Trek* TV series), and the parents of Olympic gold medalist Kristi Yamaguchi. When given the opportunity to serve their country, 1,256 *nisei* (second-generation Japanese-Americans) volunteered to join the 100th Battalion, made up completely of Americans of Japanese ancestry (AJAs). The battalion was shipped overseas in late 1943 and saw heavy action in Italy. The following year, the 100th was absorbed by the "Go for Broke" 442nd Regimental Combat Team, composed of AJAs from Hawaii and the U.S. mainland. The 442nd, whose members earned more than 18,000 individual decorations, including 9,486 Purple Hearts, was the most decorated unit of World War II.

In terms of lives lost (both military and civilian) and property damage, the Second World War was the costliest in history. The United States fought the war on two fronts, in Europe and in the Pacific, absorbing enormous casualties and exacting ferocious revenge against the Japanese. In his book *Scapegoats: A Defense of Kimmel and Short at Pearl Harbor,* Edward L. Beach described the effect that the Pearl Harbor attack had on a nation that once thought itself indestructible: "At Pearl Harbor, in a single move, Japan greatly embarrassed [the United States] as a nation. It did major damage to our defense establishment, offended our national pride in general, and shattered our self-assurance. . . . Never was a shock more devastating, or more global in scope. Nor was there ever one more destructive to the perpetrator."

So high ran the emotions of U.S. servicemen that exacting revenge became a matter of hitting the Japanese with a bomb for every one they had dropped on Pearl Harbor—and then some. And finally, on August 6 and 9, 1945, the United States dropped two atomic bombs on the Japanese cities of Hiroshima and Nagasaki, killing as many as 200,000 people and nearly obliterating the cities themselves. With these bombs the world realized that mankind had acquired the means to destroy itself.

Reflections still come some 60 years after the 1941 attack on Pearl Harbor. Former Japanese diplomat Yuzuru Sanematsu expresses a sentiment shared by many of his countrymen: "When I look back on the past the first thing I think is that it was such a high price to pay to learn a lesson about peace. And, it should never be repeated." A similar statement—and one that still resonates today—came from President Franklin Roosevelt. "I have seen war," he said. "I have seen war on land and sea. I have seen blood running from the wounded. I have seen the dead in the mud. I have seen cities destroyed. I have seen children starving. I have seen the agony of mothers and wives. I hate war."

Chronology

1854	Commodore Matthew C. Perry forces Japan to open its doors to foreign trade.
1867	The Meiji Restoration begins.
1880s	Japanese begin migrating to the Hawaiian Islands.
1894–95	Japan goes to war with China over Korea; Japan wins the war but, under pressure from other countries, ultimately relinquishes control of the Liaotung Peninsula to China.
1896	Russia and China sign a 15-year agreement in which Russia is permitted to build the Chinese Eastern Railroad through northern Manchuria.
1898	The United States annexes Hawaii and the Philippine Islands.
1904–05	The Japanese Imperial Navy attacks the Russian fleet at Port Arthur on February 8, 1904, sparking the Russo-Japanese War; the 1905 Treaty of Portsmouth ends the war and grants Japan control of the Liaotung Peninsula, southern Sakhalin, and Korea.
1914	World War I breaks out; Japan has a minor role on the side of the Allied forces.
1927	Japan begins sinking into an economic depression.
1931–32	Japan provokes a conflict with China in an attempt to seize Manchuria. The Chinese are defeated and Japan annexes the region despite censure from the League of Nations.
1937	Japanese troops engage the Chinese at the Marco Polo Bridge near Peking (now Beijing) on July 7, launching another war against China; this second Sino-Japanese War lasts eight years.
1939	Germany invades Poland on September 1, igniting World War II.
1940	U.S. Pacific Fleet departs for Hawaii on April 10; Germany defeats France in June; Japan signs Tripartite Pact and forms Axis alliance with Germany and Italy on September 27. The United States suspends shipments of vital resources to Japan and deliberately allows its trade treaty with the Japanese to expire.

Chronology

1941   In February, the Japanese begin a feasibility study for a possible surprise attack on Pearl Harbor; by June, Japanese aerial units are running practice maneuvers off the island of Kyushu. On October 12, Japanese officials agree to continue making preparations for war while still in negotiations with the United States; Japan begins deploying forces for an attack in mid-November. On December 7, despite last-minute attempts at negotiation, the Imperial Japanese Fleet attacks the U.S. Pacific Fleet at Pearl Harbor. The attack devastates the naval base; including civilians, between 2,388 and 2,403 Americans are killed, and 1,178 are wounded. The following day, the United States declares war on Japan and enters World War II.

1942   On February 19, Roosevelt orders that, "by virtue of their racial similarity to the enemy," all Japanese men, women, and children living in America be evacuated from their homes and placed in internment camps. More than 110,000 Japanese, most of them American citizens, are relocated.

1945   On August 6 and 9, the United States drops atomic bombs on Hiroshima and Nagasaki, Japan. The Japanese surrender to the United States aboard the USS *Missouri* on September 2.

Bibliography

Beach, Edward L. *Scapegoats: A Defense of Kimmel and Short at Pearl Harbor.* Annapolis, Md.: Naval Institute Press, 1995.

Goldstein, Donald M.; Katherine V. Dillon; and J. Michael Wenger. *The Way It Was: Pearl Harbor—The Original Photographs.* Dulles, Va.: Brassey, Inc., 1995.

Hoyt, Edwin P. *Japan's War.* New York: Da Capo Press, Inc., 1989.

Landay, Jonathan S. "Officers Join Effort to Exonerate Pearl Harbor Commanders." *Philadelphia Inquirer,* 24 November 1999.

Lenihan, Daniel J. "The *Arizona* Revisited: Divers Explore the Legacy of Pearl Harbor." *Natural History,* November 1991. On National Park Service's Submerged Cultural Resources Unit website (http://www.nps.gov/scru/revisit2.html)

Lord, Walter. *Day of Infamy.* Hertfordshire, England: Wordsworth Editions Limited, 1998.

McComas, Terence. *Pearl Harbor: Fact and Reference Book—Everything to Know About December 7, 1941.* Honolulu: Mutual Publishing, 1991.

Meyer, Milton W. *Japan: A Concise History.* Lanham, Md.: Rowan and Littlefield Publishers, Inc., 1993.

Prange, Gordon W. *At Dawn We Slept.* New York: McGraw-Hill, 1981.

Slackman, Michael. *Remembering Pearl Harbor: The Story of the USS Arizona Memorial.* Honolulu: Arizona Memorial Museum Association, 1998.

————. *Target: Pearl Harbor.* Honolulu: University of Hawaii Press, 1991.

Takaki, Ronald. *Strangers from a Different Shore.* New York: Little, Brown and Co., 1989.

Taylor, Theodore. *Air Raid—Pearl Harbor! The Story of December 7, 1941.* New York: Harcourt Brace, 1991.

Walton, Mary. "Paradise Lost." *Philadelphia Inquirer Magazine,* 1 December 1991.

Bibliography

WEBSITES

Arizona Memorial Museum Association
http://www.weblane.com/arizonamemorial

Hawaii Guide
http://www.hawaiiguide.com/history.htm

> Brief overview of the Pearl Harbor area, the 1941 Japanese attack on the U.S. Pacific Fleet, and the USS *Arizona* battleship and the memorial that spans her sunken hull

National Park Service: Explore Your National Parks—Historic Places
http://www.cr.nps.gov/nr/twhp/curriculumkit/lessons/arizona

> A curriculum kit about the attack on Pearl Harbor, including site maps, readings, images, and teaching activities

National Park Service: The USS *Arizona* Memorial
http://www.nps.gov/usar/

> Photos, visitation information, and an extended site that gives details about the memorial and about the attack and destruction of the *Arizona*

Submerged Cultural Resources Unit
http://www.nps.gov/scru/home.htm

University of Arizona Library
http://www.library.arizona.edu/images/USS_Arizona/history/history.html

Index

Index

Index

Picture Credits

JUDY L. HASDAY, a native of Philadelphia, Pennsylvania, received her B.A. in communications and her Ed.M. in instructional technologies from Temple University. A multimedia professional, she has had her photographs published in several magazines and books. As a successful freelance author, Ms. Hasday has written several books, including an award-winning biography of James Earl Jones and biographies of Madeleine Albright and Tina Turner. She also coauthored *Marijuana,* a book that presents to adolescents the facts about and dangers of using the drug.

JILL McCAFFREY has served for four years as national chairman of the Armed Forces Emergency Services of the American Red Cross. Ms. McCaffrey also serves on the board of directors for Knollwood—the Army Distaff Hall. The former Jill Ann Faulkner, a Massachusetts native, is the wife of Barry R. McCaffrey, a member of President Bill Clinton's cabinet and director of the White House Office of National Drug Control Policy. The McCaffreys are the parents of three grown children: Sean, a major in the U.S. Army; Tara, an intensive care nurse and captain in the National Guard; and Amy, a seventh grade teacher. The McCaffreys also have two grandchildren, Michael and Jack.